FASCIST

ITALY

Second
Edition

FASCIST ITALY
Second Edition

Alan Cassels

McMaster University

Harlan Davidson, Inc.
Wheeling, Illinois 60090-6000

Library of Congress Cataloging in Publication Data
Cassels, Alan., 1929—
    Fascist Italy.

    (Europe since 1500 series)
    Bibliography: p. 121
    Includes index.
    1. Fascism—Italy—History. 2. Italy—History—
1922–1945. I. Title. II. Series.
DG571.C425   1985   320.5'33
84-21485
ISBN 0-88295-828-3

For My Parents

Contents

Preface to the Second Edition

In the fifteen years since the original composition of this brief work, much inevitably has been published on Fascism at large and Italian Fascism in particular. However, whereas it has grown increasingly difficult to discern a dialectical shape in the war of words which swirls around generic Fascism, the debate over Italian Fascism has continued during the past two decades to be developed largely within a familiar context. Two basic questions are still asked of Fascism in Italy. The first concerns its place in the history of united Italy; was Fascism an outgrowth or a breach of Italy's national traditions? The Italian national conscience remains sorely perplexed on this score even after half a century of discussion. The other issue has to do with the substance of Italian Fascism; did it ever possess a set of coherent ideas and practices, or was it just a vehicle of Mussolini's opportunism, extreme Italian nationalism, or vested interests of the country's propertied classes? This question, especially, continues to supply ammunition for argument in intellectual quarters. Since these two durable problems provided the conceptual and historiographical framework of this book's first edition, I have seen no reason to change the overall format here.

On the other hand, recent literature has sought to fill the factual gaps in our knowledge of Italian Fascism, and has tended to dwell on those aspects formerly overlooked or undervalued. For example, Fascism's emergence and swift capture of power in the early 1920s has been illuminated by a series of regional case histories. The Fascist impact on Italian life in the next decade has been usefully examined through several studies of the younger generation and education. These, in turn, have sparked some interest in the vestigial idealism of the Fascist movement (as opposed to the atrophy of the regime), and in corporativism as a theoretical "third way" between capitalism and socialism. But unquestionably the major publicity over the past few years has attached to the suggestion made by Italy's leading authority on the Fascist era, Renzo De Felice, that Mussolini, at least between 1929 and 1936, achieved a veritable consensus of support among the Italian population. Even Italy's press, radio, and television briefly took up this bone of contention. Elsewhere in the field of Mussolinian biography, the tendency of late has been to offset the Duce's more clownish traits by a stress on his cruelty and relish for war. All these fresh emphases, perspectives, and variations on older themes I have tried to build into this revised edition. The latest scholarship is more specifically indicated in the updated bibliographical references in the text, as well as in a new bibliographical essay.

Introduction

Not without good reason, the years in Europe embraced by the two world wars have sometimes been called the epoch of fascism. Italian Fascism might thus be regarded merely as one facet of a supranational phenomenon. Unfortunately, however, it is not easy to reach a clear definition of *universalfascismo*. In an article pointedly called "What Fascism Is Not," *American Historical Review* (1979), Gilbert Allardyce comes close to denying any meaning whatsoever to the concept of fascism. At the other extreme, A. J. Gregor in several political science tomes stretches the meaning of fascism so far as to include a number of Third World developmental dictatorships. A wiser consensus follows a middle path. This holds that every fascist movement, while emerging out of the same crisis of Western liberalism and capitalism and sharing a common addiction to authoritarianism and nationalism, also betrayed its own distinct idiosyncracies. On the one hand, Italian Fascism was a part of *universalfascismo*, and indeed a fascist prototype admired and imitated around the globe in the 1920s and 1930s. On the other hand, Italy's brand of fascism was neither alone nor least in possessing a peculiar national character. For this latter reason—and out of considerations of space—this book concentrates on Fascist Italy per se. International fascism is not totally disregarded, but, when considered, it is primarily to illustrate the Italian story.

Broadly speaking, there are two ways of looking at the Fascist episode in Italian history between 1922 and 1943. One is to regard it as a gigantic confidence trick perpetrated on the Italian nation by

Benito Mussolini, a view once advanced out of political necessity. In the United States during the Second World War, it was deemed wise to assure the Italo-American segment of the electorate that war was being waged, not on the Italian people but on a regime alien to Italy's traditions. In the same vein, Winston Churchill appealed to the Italian people themselves over the head of the "one man alone" responsible for leading his country to disaster "against the wishes of the Italian people, who had no lust for this war." After 1945, Italian patriots tried to rehabilitate their nation's fallen reputation by cultivating the notion that Fascism had been a temporary aberration in Italian history. Such was the "parenthesis thesis," propagated most notably by Benedetto Croce. From all this, it followed that the whole story of Fascism could be subsumed in a biography of Mussolini. In fact, this has been the most popular approach. Most people remain untouched by the academic denigration of the "great man" theory of history and find it quite credible that one man, with a few cronies, captured an entire nation and moved it to action. By popular repute, Mussolini was *il Duce* (the Leader) in fact as well as name. So the biographies of Mussolini, ranging inordinately in quality, have rolled off the presses without stop.

The other approach to Italian Fascism, a product of modern scholarship and so more deterministic, views Fascism less as an artificial creation of Mussolini than a direct outgrowth of Italian history. Environment shaped the rise and success of Fascism, not the reverse; Mussolini is demoted to an agent of a historical force. This is the clear inference to be drawn from the manifold scholarly investigations into pre-Fascist Italy; avowed or not, they are quests for the roots of Fascism in traditional Italian society. In this context, Fascism triumphed because it responded to the needs of that society; this interpretation has been labeled the "revelation thesis."

The historical truth must, of course, combine biography with deep societal trends. Appropriately, the most ambitious biography of Mussolini, as yet uncompleted by Renzo De Felice, is advertised as a conscious attempt to relate the Duce to his background; to insert him, in the author's words, "in a fan-like perspective which opens up gradually as Mussolini's horizons broaden." This present essay on Fascist Italy will similarly try to steer a central course.

Whether one equates Mussolini with Fascism or associates Fascism with the mainstream of Italian history, one cannot simply begin the narrative in the year 1922. Mussolini was a well-known political figure long before he became premier, and his early career had a crucial bearing on his conduct in office. From the other interpretative standpoint, if one holds that Fascism was the realization of long-standing Italian tendencies, it is even more incumbent to say something of pre-Fascist Italy. Such is the purpose behind the first sections of this book, which try to set the stage for Fascism's actual attainment of power in 1922.

It is easier to designate an end than a beginning to the history of Fascist Italy. The end came in two precise stages. On July 25, 1943, King Victor Emmanuel III dismissed Mussolini, and with this move, Fascist Italy, strictly speaking, ceased to exist. However, for nearly two years after his dismissal, Mussolini continued to operate a ramshackle Fascist regime in the North, until he was caught by his enemies and killed on April 28, 1945. His end was almost simultaneous with the close of the Second World War in Europe, which thus conveniently marked the demise of Fascism as a mode of government anywhere in Italy.

1
The Background

Between 1859 and 1870, the Italian peninsula was united into a single nation-state, an accomplishment for which popular enthusiasm and participation were not totally lacking. Nevertheless, the majority of the Italian population either remained unmoved or else were positively alienated by the new unitary state. Unification was the ambition chiefly of a vigorous upper-middle-class minority of Italians. Yet even this minority, which at once assumed control of united Italy, had not really brought it into existence. This had been done, in the last resort, by French and Prussian armies, which resulted in a sense of national shame on the part of the ruling class of the new Italy. From these two factors—the gulf between the state and the masses and a national inferiority complex—nearly all of Italy's troubles have stemmed.

United Italy began life with a typical nineteenth-century liberal constitution, which comprised a monarchy of limited powers, and a bicameral legislature made up of an appointed senate and a chamber of deputies elected on a narrow property franchise. With the passage of time, ministries grew less dependent on the monarch's favor and more on that of the elected lower house of the legislature. The drift toward parliamentary sovereignty was a familiar process in nineteenth-century Europe. On the other hand, the Italian parliamentary system was conspicuous for its failure to develop clearly defined, viable political parties—a circumstance that placed a serious obstacle in the way of building a stable parliamentary majority able to keep a government in office for any length of time. The

5

problem was met, if not exactly solved, by a series of parliamentary managers, who displayed prodigious skill in fashioning majorities out of the amorphous mass of deputies seated in the center of the chamber. By this method of *trasformismo* (transformism), as it was called, various shades of political opinion were included within a parliamentary majority or government. Indeed, for transformism to work at all it was necessary to suppress, or at least disguise, divisions of parliamentary opinion. Thus, one ministry came to look very much like another in principles and personnel; it was consensus politics carried to the ultimate.

Lacking the weapon of party discipline, Italy's political leaders turned to the distribution of favors in order to secure a parliamentary majority. This occurred during national elections, especially in rural areas where the traditional power structure was in a position to deliver a bloc vote. Between elections and within the Chamber of Deputies, members were manipulated in myriad ways: by the bestowal of an important office on a deputy (or a deputy's friend or relation), by the location of a public works project in a member's district, or by an introduction into the lucrative world of speculative finance. The entire process gave abundant opportunity for venality, which indeed became endemic. The aura of corruption, together with the lack of any real political debate, hardly endeared the parliamentary regime to the mass of Italians. Some were indignant at scandals; most affected a resigned indifference to national politics.

Nor did the parliamentary regime's handling of serious economic and social problems do anything to repair its public image. The very unification of Italy was regarded as such a tremendous feat that of itself it would cure all the peninsula's ailments. The evasion of awkward truths was nowhere better illustrated than in the South or *Mezzogiorno*. Barren, poverty-stricken, savage, and almost a foreign country to the northerners who wielded greatest influence in Rome, the South impeded Italy's every step on the road to national unity and material progress. Official inquiries were commissioned and reported on the southern plight, sometimes graphically. Yet, parliamentary interest remained feeble. Governments addressed themselves only to the symptoms of the *Mezzogiorno* question—peasant uprisings that were put down with ferocity. The most notorious disturbances occurred in the early 1890s in Sicily, where the rebels took on a time-honored name for workers' groups—*fasci*. Francesco Crispi, the premier and parliamentary dictator responsible for repression in this case, was a Sicilian by birth. He too refused to entertain the idea that the southern peasantry might have justifiable grievances against their lot; instead, he conceived the bizarre explanation that their discontent was attributable to agents of the Russan Tsar.

Industrialization added another dimension to Italy's socioeconomic problem. The proletariat which congregated rapidly in the northern towns was exploited as grossly as anywhere else in Europe. Parliament proved as insensitive to the new urban slums as to old-fashioned rural poverty. Crispi invoked martial law against northern strikers and Sicilian *fasci* with complete impartiality, and in 1894 he won parliamentary authority to outlaw the infant Socialist party.

In the threatening struggle between haves and have-nots, the Roman politicians were overwhelmingly on the side of property. In a way, this was merely a reflection of the fact that the governmental and business worlds overlapped. A large segment of the Italian business community was involved in the influence-peddling that was the parliamentary way of life—a condition dramatically illustrated in a series of bank scandals uncovered in 1889, which concerned the illegal overissue of currency by the banks and the bribery of ministers and deputies to tolerate it. The most startling aspect of the affair was not the nexus revealed between bankers and politicos, nor even the corruptibility of both, but the action of the Chamber of Deputies which voted to keep secret the report of financial irregularities; it was three years before the yellow press exposed the scandal to the public and prodded parliament and the courts into action. It was no accident that the Italians Gaetano Mosca and Vilfredo Pareto, drawing on their acquaintance with the contemporary political scene in Rome, should be among the first social scientists to formulate a theory of self-perpetuating elites. Toward the close of the nineteenth century, the Italian parliament seemed to serve primarily the interests of a wealthy elite. As a means of reconciling the masses to the united state of Italy, the parliamentary regime was proving an almost total failure.

In international affairs no less than domestic the liberal governments failed to deliver what was expected. In 1881, France seized the North African territory of Tunisia from under the nose of the Italians, who had been accustomed to regard it as an Italian zone of influence. Whereupon in a fit of pique at France, Italy applied to join the Austro-German alliance. This being granted, many upper-class Italians saw fit to embark on a slavish imitation of German fashions—in art and scholarship, in political and economic philosophy, and so on—a depressing foretaste of what was to happen fifty years later as a result of the fascist Rome-Berlin Axis. Italian subservience to the Austro-German bloc was further proclaimed by Rome's soft-pedaling of the Trentino and Trieste issues. These regions on Italy's frontiers were heavily Italian-speaking, but still lived under the rule of the Habsburg Empire. They constituted Italy's principal *terre irredente* (unredeemed lands) and the prime object of Italian patriotic passion, which now had to be muted for *raison d'état*. Italy's rather ignominious position in world affairs was crowned when Crispi resolved to distract attention from troubles at home by launching a colonial attack on Ethiopia (or Abyssinia, its Arabic name often used in the ages of imperialism). The outcome was a fiasco. In 1896, at Adowa, 6,000 Italian troops were lost, and the conquest of Ethiopia was deferred until Mussolini pursued it forty years later. If Italy had emerged from the process of unification with a national inferiority complex, the record of the parliamentary regime's foreign policy only served to aggravate the condition.

By the close of the nineteenth century, the shortcomings of the parliamentary regime had grown so flagrant as to threaten the political structure itself. Between 1898 and 1900, conservative groups of an authoritarian stamp undertook a studied campaign to reverse the trend toward parliamentary sovereignty. The heart of the effort lay in certain "exceptional laws" proposed by a right-wing ministry headed by a military man, General Pelloux. These exceptional laws aimed at curtailing the constitutional liberties of free speech and assembly; if passed, they would have drastically reduced any government's accountability to parliament and the judiciary on a permanent basis. (By contrast, Crispi had gone outside the law only in a spasmodic, *ad hoc* manner.) In proportion as ministries would be relieved of the need to build parliamentary majorities by bribery, they would revert to dependence on the Crown as the original Italian constitution intended. The primary purpose in freeing the hands of the executive, whether royal or ministerial or both, was to permit summary action against the strikers and rioters in the northern cities. But it was also calculated that a strong and incorrupt government at home would be a strong one abroad; thus Adowa would be revenged.

When an attempt was made to put these ideas into practice, this conservative experiment failed. True, with royal support and by the usual method of buying votes, Pelloux was able to win a majority for his scheme in the Chamber of Deputies. On the other hand, the opposition banded together in a display of unity rare in Italian politics and began to talk in unfamiliar parliamentary language of the sanctity of law and parliamentary rights. The opposition filibustered; then, in imitation of the ancient Roman plebs' gesture of protest—withdrawal to the neighboring Aventine Hills—the opposition deputies en masse walked out of the chamber. This was the government's opportunity; now the exceptional laws could be approved by the rump assembly. Of course, this would have been tantamount to a *coup d'état;* and as the issue had roused popular emotions to an extent unseen since the capture of Rome in 1870, civil war might have followed. Faced with this possibility, the Right lost its courage. In a supreme anticlimax, Pelloux quietly resigned, and a more moderate and transformist government was created. The parliamentary regime thus gained a reprieve, but the writing on the wall was clear. An alternative to parliamentary government had been seriously proposed: a strong executive, above corruption and the law, to suppress unrest at home and assert Italy's interests abroad. Later, this was the Fascist program in outline. Indeed the Fascists were to offer much of what the traditional Italian Right failed to accomplish in 1900.

In the short run, the parliamentary system appeared to gain from the constitutional crisis. A good deal of public support had rallied to it under attack, and there was a general expectation that the liberals had been frightened into correcting its worst abuses. It was almost like a bright new beginning for united Italy. In point of fact, the optimism did not prove wholly misplaced. A positive attempt was made to remove the impression that parliament spoke only for narrow interest groups. In most labor disputes the government, instead of lending police and military support to the employers, now adopted a hands-off policy. Consequently, some ministries in the first decade of the new century even received some socialist backing. But the most daring stratagem to reconcile the Italian masses to the political system was the promulgation in 1912 of virtual manhood suffrage, an act increasing from three million to eight and a half million the number of Italians entitled to participate in the political process.

Such progressive measures were largely the work of Giovanni Giolitti, who held sway over a succession of ministries between 1901 and the outbreak of the First World War. Modern scholarship has tended to sympathize with Giolitti's difficulties and to applaud his modest accomplishments. However, there are two sides to the Giolittian picture, and there remains much substance in the charge of an older school of thought that Giolitti's reforms were too few and even self-serving. For one thing, he ignored the problem of the South and preferred to use that unreconstructed region as a power base. Some critics charged that the law of 1912 was deliberately calculated to enfranchise the southern peasantry whose votes were easily controlled by the Giolittian machine. Giolitti was, in fact, an old-fashioned parliamentary manager, who governed by conventional and corrupt means. The famous Italian historian, Gaetano

Salvemini, a contemporary antagonist of Giolitti, characterized him as *"il ministro della mala vita"* (minister of vice), not so much for what he did with power but for how he obtained and retained it. The perpetuation of old, tainted methods, after the expectation of something better, rekindled a popular mood of cynicism toward the political process. In this manner, Giolitti blunted the favorable impact of his enlightened policies on labor and the suffrage, while contributing fatefully to that steady debasement of the parliamentary regime which ultimately opened the door to Fascism.

Giolitti was an unwitting precursor of Fascism in another way. The Italian Nationalist Association was founded in 1910 and proceeded to coordinate a burgeoning agitation to seize Libya in North Africa by fighting Turkey. Giolitti, who argued that Libya was Italy's by "historical fatality," succumbed willingly to Nationalist pressure. The Italo-Turkish war of 1911–1912 was less glorious and more costly than anticipated in Rome, but withal, Italy emerged decisively victorious. However, the appetite proverbially grows with eating, and the Nationalists demanded extension of the war and criticized the peace treaty that gave Libya to Italy. More important, this criticism spilled over into a blanket indictment of the liberal politicians and regime. How, it was asked, could a noble ideal like national honor be entrusted to those who were so mercenary in their daily business? How could energetic diplomacy and swift military action be expected from a debating society? Such questions were asked—and answered negatively—not only by the Nationalist Association and party, but also by many not formally inscribed as nationalists at all. An influential artistic coterie, the Futurists, made it stylish to decry arid liberalism and exalt the search for national honor by war. Nationalism was a tiger on whose back Giolitti had chosen to ride; now it threatened to devour him and the system he cherished.

The assertion of an incompatibility between parliamentarianism and the national spirit was enhanced during the First World War. At first, Italy refused to fight alongside her nominal Austro-German allies and remained neutral, but within nine months, she joined the war on the opposite side. This reversal of alliances and entry into war were hardly orthodox governmental decisions. The Treaty of London of April 26, 1915, which bound Italy to the Anglo-French bloc, was negotiated mainly at the king's behest. The parliament was called into session to obtain its endorsement of a declaration of war which, if not constitutionally necessary, would create an impression of national unity. The majority of deputies were against intervention. Many of them took their cue from Giolitti who, although no longer in office, still wielded vast influence. And Giolitti, cautious in foreign policy after his earlier brush with the forces of nationalism, was a convinced neutralist in 1915. His argument was simply that the Austro-Germans could be brought to pay almost as much for Italy's neutrality as the Anglo-French for her intervention. Indeed, before parliament met, Vienna publicly offered substantial concessions in the Trentino and Trieste. Yet, the Giolittian neutralist majority melted almost overnight. At its first meeting, without knowing the exact terms of the Treaty of London, the Chamber of Deputies voted for war by over a five-to-one margin; the Senate's vote was unanimous. Parliament was, in fact, coerced—by the king and even more by nationalist mobs that staged unruly demonstrations in the piazzas of major cities. (In a few years they would be Fascist mobs.) The burden of the street propaganda was that it was undignified for a major power not to fight. Which side Italy joined was less important than joining the war for its own sake. Intervention betrayed a growing habit of mind in Italy to give priority to action at the expense of thought; under the Fascists this was to be elevated into a dogma.

The parliamentary regime, having accepted the war against its better judgment, as it were, soon came under fire for maladministration of the war effort and for the inevitable mass misery of war. The war was indeed run ineptly from Rome, although no more so than it was from London and Paris. However, the Italian record was made to seem worse by the disaster of Caporetto in November 1917, when the Italian armies in the northeast were rolled back a hundred miles in three weeks. Actually, Caporetto resulted only in part from specific blunders by both civil and military authorities. It testified just as much to the low state of Italian morale, for the war was not popular among the people—an indication that the interventionist campaign of 1915 had been that of a noisy minority. After Caporetto, an upsurge of patriotism did affect nearly all Italians, but this was a spontaneous reaction to the danger of Austrian penetration into the heart of Italy; the exhortations of the politicians in Rome counted for relatively little. The regime was thus held responsible for Italy's wartime failures but not the final victory. For this reason alone, historians have agreed that the parliamentary system emerged from the war with stature still further diminished in the eyes of the Italian people.

Over a half-century of liberal, parliamentary government had not resolved Italy's two pristine difficulties. The divorce between nation and state remained; the making of Italy had not been followed by the making of Italians. Manhood suffrage was too recent to have had much effect, and the post-Caporetto patriotism proved a transient phenomenon. The mass of Italians were perhaps even more estranged from the state in 1918 than in 1861; certainly many illusions had perished in the interim. As for the other fundamental problem—that of gaining respect among the nations—the Italian performance in the scramble for Africa and in the world war was uneven and mediocre at best. Of course, national prestige was mostly an upper- and middle-class preoccupation, but then these classes in 1918 still generated the preponderance of articulate political opinion. When Mussolini launched his Fascist movement in March 1919, his program was tailored exactly to provide answers to Italy's two unresolved problems. Integral nationalism, the essence of Fascism, postulated as total an identification of the Italian people with the state as possible. And this would be the means to an end— that of asserting the national will abroad.

Italy 1918–1945

2
The Opportunity

Benito Amilcare Andrea Mussolini was born the eldest in a family of three children on July 29, 1883, at Predappio, a small town in the region of east-central Italy called the Romagna. His place of birth was a major influence in determining his character. The Romagna was renowned for its tradition of rebellion against constituted authority, and Mussolini was brought up a true Romagnole. His blacksmith father, an outspoken anticlerical republican and socialist, named him Benito after the Mexican revolutionary Juarez, and Amilcare Andrea after the Italian socialists Cipriani and Costa. It was from his father that Benito acquired his hatred of all who enjoyed privilege by birth. For his mother, who was a pious and conformist elementary schoolteacher, he had a sentimental affection, but his father he respected and imitated. He displayed his resentment of the established order early. When he was nine, his mother saved enough of her meager salary to send him to the Salesian Fathers' school in nearby Faenza. There he was made to feel the shame of poverty; with others who paid the minimum rate of fees he ate inferior food at segregated tables in the dining hall. The young Mussolini fought the religious institution at every turn, once throwing an inkpot at a teacher who tried to cane him with a ruler. In his second year, he stabbed a richer schoolmate with a pocketknife, whereupon he was expelled. His distrust and dislike of the privileged classes were muted later in life—after all, he cooperated with them—but these feelings never entirely left him.

Mussolini's early career was a checkered one. After his brush

15

with the Salesian Fathers, he was sent to a lay school in Forlimpopoli. Despite further acts of indiscipline and another knife incident, he graduated in 1902 with a certificate to teach in elementary school. However, he never held any teaching position for longer than a year. Indeed, he gave up his first post within a few months to try his luck in Switzerland. First, he undertook manual labor and discovered how shamefully Italian immigrants were exploited. Next, he had recourse to begging, was arrested, and experienced his first taste of prison. After three weeks, he appealed for help to a group of Italian socialists in a Lausanne café. They took him in, and from then on his passion in life became, like that of his father before him, political agitation. For some two years, by lecturing and writing in proletarian journals, Mussolini joined in the campaign to organize Italian immigrant labor in Switzerland, in the process coming into contact with some of the luminaries of international socialism. Two in particular befriended him at this time: Angelica Balabanov, a Russian emigré, tried in a motherly fashion to school him in socialist doctrine; Giacinto Serrati, an Italian recently fled from the United States, was later instrumental in Mussolini's progress in the socialist movement. Mussolini returned to Italy in 1904 to perform his obligatory term of military service, and then came another stint as schoolmaster. But in 1908, his friends secured for him the editorship of an Italian socialist paper in the Austrian city of Trent. Mussolini plunged into the work vigorously and in eight months the Austrians expelled him. In socialist eyes, his expulsion was testimony to his zeal, and he was not long out of a job. He was invited to become secretary of the Socialist federation in his native province of Forlì, and also to found a local weekly journal. This appeared in 1910 under the title *La Lotta di Classe* (*The Class Struggle*), and represented Mussolini's own work from start to finish. Given a free rein, he was not long in establishing an ascendancy over the Forlì Socialists. At the same time, he used this local power base to project himself on to the national scene.

Like most European Socialist parties of the time, the *Partito socialista italiana* (P.S.I.) was split down the middle. The reformists were prepared to work for the immediate alleviation of the workers' lot, even at the risk of delaying the day of true revolution. This meant participation in a bourgeois parliamentary system and, within parliament, pressure on a middle-class government to make concessions to labor. In the Italian context, it meant pragmatic support of Giolitti because his social policy was an improvement on what had gone before. On the other hand, the revolutionaries, who liked to regard themselves as orthodox Marxists, held to the view that socialism could only be achieved by a violent assault on the capitalist system. To them, all compromise with the enemy for short-term gains was treason. For most of the Giolilttian era, the revisionists held sway within the P.S.I., but when Giolitti embarked on the Libyan War of 1911, he undercut his allies in the Socialist party. Imperialism was anathema to practically all Socialists, and its adoption seemed to justify the revolutionaries' hard line.

There had never been any doubt where Mussolini stood in the reformist-revolutionary controversy. He was an extremist and consistently urged violence as a means of change. He persuaded the Forlì Socialists to secede from the P.S.I. between 1910 and 1912 because of the party's reformist leadership. As a result, he fitted in easily with the orthodox Marxists, which is not to say that he himself was a Marxist, despite Balabanov's tutoring. Although he liked to pretend to be well read, he was, in the words of Denis Mack Smith's acerbic biography (1982), "an intellectual poseur and cultural exhibitionist . . . [whose] particular skill was to pick up ideas almost at random if they coincided with some prejudice or tactical need." Thus, he acknowledged a debt to Sorel and Nietzsche because they scorned weakness and sanctioned force. In reality, Mussolini's advocacy of violent revolution was an expression of his personal hatred of middle-class Italy.

Like other revolutionary socialists, Mussolini vehemently denounced nationalism as a capitalist trait and a bourgeois snare to entrap the workers. He gained notoriety by echoing the sentiment of the French socialist, Gustave Hervé, that "the flag is a rag to be planted on the dunghill." During his brief stay in the Trentino, he had worked with Italian irredentists of a left-wing stamp, but he had always held aloof from their nationalist agitation. Later, when a nationalist leader himself, Mussolini would pretend to have been expelled from the Trentino because of his irredentism; actually he had been expelled for his anticlericalism. On the outbreak of the Libyan War, Mussolini turned to sabotage, and in 1911–1912 he spent five months in prison for fomenting riots in Forlì which had impeded public transport carrying reserves called into the army. In July 1912, Mussolini attended the national congress of the P.S.I. at Reggio Emilia. There, rank-and-file revulsion against cooperation with the Giolittian government, sharpened by the Libyan colonial episode, was obvious from the start. The revolutionary wing chose Mussolini, something of a hero after his recent imprisonment and known for his power of invective, to lead the vendetta against the reformist leadership. He fulfilled this task with gusto. Largely as a result of his bitter attack, Leonida Bissolati and three other prominent moderates were ejected from the party, and the revolutionary socialists gained control of the Executive Committee. Mussolini was rewarded for his services with the editorship of the Milan daily, *Avanti (Forward)*, the official voice of Italian socialism. Thus, Mussolini reached prominence in the wake of the nationalist furor over Libya; henceforth, too, Italian nationalism was to act as the great determinant of his career.

He was a successful editor of *Avanti* for almost two years; circulation jumped from 28,000 to 94,000. His editorials were essays in revolutionary socialism, calling for a general strike at the slightest sign of working-class unrest. Naturally, when war broke out in 1914, it was depicted as "the extreme form of class collaboration, the annihilation of individual autonomy and the freedom of thought, which are sacrificed to state and militarism." *Avanti's* readers were exhorted to be "neutral as proletarians, neutral as Italians." However, the rumor soon began to circulate that Mussolini was about to desert the cause of nonintervention, although it was generally discounted by his socialist colleagues. To them, it was a bombshell when he announced his defection on October 18, 1914. On that date, *Avanti* carried a lengthy editorial entitled "From Absolute Neutrality to Active and Operative Neutrality." Under this rubric, Mussolini distinguished between the democratic Entente states and the autocratic Central Powers, and he advocated Italian favoritism of the former even up to the point of intervention. Not content with breaching the principle of international proletarian solidarity, Mussolini flirted with the argument most despised by socialists—that of national honor: "We enjoy the extraordinary privilege of living at the most tragic hour of the world's history. Do we wish to be—as men and Socialists—inert spectators of this grandiose drama? Or would we prefer to be, in some way, its protagonists?"

Mussolini was, in fact, following the broad path that many syndicalist socialists, like Filippo Corridoni and Michele Bianchi, had already taken in August 1914. These interpreted the war as an ideological struggle between the international Right symbolized by Germany and the Left represented by the Anglo-French. Therefore, the Italian proletariat could in good conscience take part in the contest—on the correct side naturally. Of greater importance, these syndicalists held that by fighting for their fatherland, the Italian workers would for the first time become integrated into the state. In this sense, the war could be made into a "revolutionary war." Here was the germ of the future Fascist idea, that of overcoming social and economic problems by a resort to nationalism. By appropriating it, Mussolini began a fruitful collaboration with the syndicalist wing of Italian socialism which lasted into the Fascist era. But the P.S.I., which had for some years ostracized the syndicalists, responded swiftly and negatively to Mussolini's syndicalist line, dismissing him, amid acrimony, from both *Avanti* and the party. Despite his new syndicalist ties, Mussolini's career as a socialist was effectively ended. Any new political role that he might assay was likely to bring him within the orbit of the Right.

Mussolini's drastic turn to intervention has been much debated and is still not capable of easy explication. Only one episode in his youth had seemed to forecast it. In 1904, profiting from an amnesty offered to draft-dodgers, Mussolini had returned from Switzerland to perform his military service. Oddly enough, in view of his violently antimilitarist pronouncements immediately before and after his term in the army, he had proved a model soldier. Once, he had written to his commanding officer requesting leave on his mother's death, and couched the letter in sentiments of unabashed patriotism. This might have been dissimulation, but it appears more likely that Mussolini found an unfamiliar but welcome sense of security within the framework of military discipline and unthinking duty. Similarly, he always adjusted contentedly to the strict regimen of prison. Mussolini was a simple soul frightened by the complexities of life. His solution was to ignore the complex and reduce matters to facile black and white terms; this accounts, of course, for his readiness to assume extreme positions. His conversion to intervention in October 1914 might be viewed as part of his search for a simplistic *Weltanschauung*. To advocate violent revolution at home and a nationalist sublimation by violence abroad attracted him by its easy if superficial consistency. The choice of violence as a criterion amounted to a triumph of means over ends; but then this had never been uncongenial to Mussolini. Now he was close to elevating violence for its own sake into a political principle.

Mussolini's enemies in 1914 and later, charged that he was bought. On November 15 appeared the first issue of Mussolini's new paper, *Popolo d'Italia (People of Italy)*. It stated bluntly: "Today antiwar propaganda is cowardice." In its early days, *Popolo d'Italia* was subsidized by Italian interventionists and the French government. But whether Mussolini had made arrangements with these backers before declaring himself in *Avanti* is very doubtful. To begin with, it is probable that he did not anticipate the need to turn elsewhere than to the P.S.I., believing his own rhetorical skill sufficient to win the party to intervention. In addition, the charge of bribery is hard to reconcile with Mussolini's complete disinterest, throughout his career, in money per se. In any event, subvention by Italian and French nationalists, which could vanish at a shift in the international situation, was scarcely a profitable exchange for the editorship of *Avanti*. For all these reasons, the historiographical consensus has been to dismiss any material motive on Mussolini's part, and instead to ascribe his apostacy to some psychological quirk that nevertheless made for a sincere conversion.

In terms of the power and influence which Mussolini craved far above money, the sincerity of his convictions cost him much. For the rest of the war, Mussolini relapsed into semiobscurity. In the crusade for intervention that he had joined, Mussolini was outshone by such long-standing nationalists as Gabriele D'Annunzio and Enrico Corradini. Mussolini's part in driving Italy into war— whatever Fascist legend might claim later—was minor. Editorials in *Popolo d'Italia* did not reach as wide an audience as those in *Avanti*, and Mussolini was only one of many arrested in street demonstrations for war. In August 1915, he was called up and spent a year and a half on active duty, of which about six months were passed in the trenches. He saw to it that his military record was recounted in heroic prose in *Popolo d'Italia*, which continued publication in Milan in his absence. But in truth, he was no more than a conscientious soldier who rose to the rank of sergeant. He was wounded quite seriously, although ingloriously, when a shell exploded inside a howitzer during firing practice. He was discharged from the hospital in the summer of 1917, in time to ride the wave of patriotism which overtook Italy after the Caporetto debacle. In the last year of the war, the British joined in providing funds for the war veteran to combat pacifism, both in his editorials and in Milanese street fights. Yet, at the war's close, patriotic agitators were supernumerary, and Mussolini was not an especially distinguished one. He had, in fact, hardly recovered from his setback in October 1914. Unlike most mortals, however, he was about to be presented with a second opportunity for fame.

In the first instance, Mussolini's fresh opportunity arose because the liberal regime creaked to a standstill. The traditional political tactics of electoral control and transformism no longer worked. Manhood suffrage introduced in 1912 had already cut deeply into them. In 1919, a broad system of proportional representation was adopted explicitly to curb the manipulation that small and single-member constituencies had lent themselves to. The day of the parliamentary manager was over; that of the mass party had arrived. From the 1919 election, two parties with grass-roots following emerged triumphant—the P.S.I. and a new Catholic party called the *Popolari* (Popular party). The salvation of the parliamentary system lay in the ability of one or the other of these two groups to supply the nucleus for a stable governmental coalition. Neither could do so.

The Socialists were still theoretical revolutionaries, which implied a rooted aversion to making parliamentary government work at all. Furthermore, the Socialist party was far too fragmented to form a solid power base. In addition to the old revolutionary-reformist cleavage, the Russian bolshevik revolution of 1917 created new questions: should the P.S.I. imitate the tactics of its Russian counterpart and even accept directives from Moscow? Ultimately, in 1921, those Socialists who answered affirmatively broke away and founded the Italian Communist party. The Popular party similarly lacked the unity needed to assume power. Its membership ranged from outright clerical reactionaries to Christian Democratic radicals. Anyway, it was always dubious whether the Vatican would allow the *Popolari* to enter a government of the secular Italian state. And perhaps needless to add, at this time ideological antipathy between Socialists and *Popolari* ran too high to permit a coalition of the moderate elements of each; to Socialists Catholicism was obscurantist, to Catholics socialism was atheistic. Therefore, by default, Italy fell back on government by transformism, although the foundations for it were eroded. The result was chronic instability. Between 1918 and 1922, five clearly distinguishable governments held office, and there were constant cabinet reshuffles between major changes. None of the postwar governments wielded sufficient authority for adequate administration.

Governmental shortcomings were particularly apparent on two fronts. First, the economic hardship caused by the reversion from a war to a civilian economy was as severe in Italy as in any other belligerent nation. Within less than two years, two and a half million demobilized soldiers were thrown on the labor market. At the same time, the gross national product and overseas trade declined rapidly. Massive unemployment ensued; the official figures, which were almost certainly an underestimation, showed a jump from ninety thousand in July 1920 to over a half-million by the end of 1921. Between 1919 and 1921, the cost of living rose by more than 50 percent. Wages rose too, quite steeply in 1920, but not all occupations benefitted, nor did the millions who lived by casual labor. Moreover, the problem was as much psychological as physical. During the war, the politicians had made extravagant promises of a brave new postwar world; unemployment and inflation were a rude awakening to reality. Disillusion was fed further by the common knowledge that not a few ruthless profiteers had made fortunes out of the war. In the circumstances, some degree of social unrest was unavoidable.

It began in the countryside of south and central Italy with peasants occupying the uncultivated fringes of large estates (*latifondi*). In the north, especially in the Po Valley, recently formed peasant leagues began a wave of agitation and strikes which, by October 1920, succeeded in winning from the landlords a collective contract which certified league hiring halls as the exclusive source of agrarian labor. But the most sensational disturbances came in the cities. In August 1920, strikers at the Alfa Romeo plant in Milan responded to a lockout by camping in the factory itself. This sit-in method of forestalling scab labor was imitated elsewhere. Yet, the experiment proved to be short-lived and the sit-ins turned out to be a peak. Afterwards, the index of discontent showed a decline. Almost eight million workdays lost by strike in 1921 was still an alarming figure, but it was less than half that of either of the two previous years. However, of greater importance than the amount of agitation was the impression it created. The central government was not only inactive but was seen to be so. Although the government acted as arbiter to bring an end to the sit-in strikes, official policy was to remain out of the battle between capital and labor. This was the convention set by Giolitti before the war, and indeed Giolitti was premier again between June 1920 and July 1921. The negative approach, once praised as impartial, now seemed merely a reflection of the government's complete inability to come up with a remedy for the conditions that caused working-class demonstrations in the first place. Traditional bread subsidies kept food prices from getting completely out of hand, but they were a terrific strain on budgets which had to cope with expenditures up to three times in excess of receipts. In turn, two premiers, Francesco Saverio Nitti and Giolitti, proposed the abolition of bread subsidies in exchange for an overhaul of the tax structure to compel the rich to assume a fairer share of the economic burden. The former suggestion alienated the Left, and the latter the Right; in the end nothing much was accomplished. There was some tinkering with the tax laws, but this was more than offset by rampant tax evasion. The combination of governmental inefficacy and the attack on property rights by rural squatters, peasant leagues, and urban sit-in strikers left Italy peculiarly susceptible to the great European fear of the time—the expectation of an imminent bolshevik coup.

The threat of bolshevism was cunningly exploited by Mussolini, and it is hard to overestimate its importance in bringing Fascism to power. Yet, in truth, the threat in Italy was almost entirely illusory. No master plan of revolution existed; peasants and workers acted without premeditation and on a local basis only. Even during the occupation of the factories, when a pattern of action seemed to emerge, there was no real cooperation between the strikers in one town and those in the next. The Socialist party signally failed to provide a national organization to take advantage of working-class distress. Whenever the P.S.I. called for a general strike, which it did more than once between 1919 and 1922, the response was halfhearted and far short of revolutionary. The Socialist leaders spent too much energy quarreling among themselves. Lenin regarded the whole Italian proletarian movement to be insufficiently mature for revolution, so no direction was forthcoming from Moscow. Furthermore, lower-class disorders and revolutionary sentiment waxed and waned, albeit not in exact accord with the fluctuations of Italy's economy. The danger years were the *"biennio rosso"* (two red years), 1919 and 1920. But by the close of the latter year, the revolutionary workers' movement was on the retreat, and a year later the worst of the postwar depression was over. By 1922, when Mussolini arrived in office claiming to save Italy from bolshevism, the threat—if ever it was there—was gone.

The other major score on which the postwar liberal regime fell short of expectations concerned foreign policy. At the Paris Peace Conference in 1919, Italy was granted status as a member of the Council of Four. Nevertheless, Britain, France, and the United States were aware of Italy's limited contribution to victory on the battlefield, and showed their disparagement in their manner and in their opposition to certain Italian demands. Irritated by this, the principal Italian delegates at one point walked out of the conference. From Paris sprang the legend that Italy's victory in 1918 had been "mutilated" in the peacemaking. The Italian public blamed the Allies for their arrogance and liberal politicians in Rome for their timidity.

In fact, Italy had little reason to feel shortchanged in the peace settlement. In 1915, Italy had gone to war with the Habsburg Empire, which three years later disintegrated entirely; few wars have ended so decisively in favor of one side. The way was open for the annexation of the traditional unredeemed lands, and on this issue the Paris Peace Conference was highly amenable. The frontier in the Tyrolean Alps was fixed to suit Italy's strategic convenience at the Brenner Pass, which consigned some 200,000 Germans to Italian rule. Moreover, unlike most other European minorities, these Germans living in the region now called the Alto Adige were granted no right of complaint to the League of Nations. Italy also got Trieste, and was offered a border with Yugoslavia that placed most of the Istrian peninsula, nearly all the strategic mountain passes, and half a million Slavs on the Italian side. These were rewards above and beyond the terms of the Treaty of London of 1915. Italian dissatisfaction arose from the Allied reluctance to fulfill wartime promises of colonial territory in Africa and the Middle East, and of a strip of Dalmatia on the eastern Adriatic shore. Italian resentment reached a crescendo at the rejection of Italy's claim to the northern Adriatic port of Fiume. The center of Fiume was Italian but its environs were Slavic. When, in 1918, Yugoslav replaced Habsburg power in the area, Italians at once became exercised about the fate of their Fiumian compatriots "amid a sea of Slavs." Unfortunately for Italy, her self-determinist claim to Fiume was vitiated by the breach of the same principle on the Brenner.

Regardless of the merits of Italy's case for colonies, Dalmatia, and Fiume, these were all subsidiary war aims; Fiume had not even been mentioned in the Treaty of London. It is very doubtful that what Italy was denied was worth having. Colonies and mandates were not automatic profit makers; on the contrary, their administration would have been a heavy expense to lay on the overburdened Italian treasury. As for Dalmatia, this was a rocky, barren region inhabited by an Italophobe people; Italian possession would most likely have meant a costly military operation with little other than prestige to win. And Fiume, so hotly contested, was an outlet for Balkan commerce; once in Italian hands, the Slavs could be expected to boycott it, making it a worthless gain. All in all, Salvemini summed up the sense of "mutilated victory" best when, in his *Prelude to World War II* (1954), he called Italy after Molière's eponymous hero the *"malade imaginaire."*

This nationalist sickness, however imaginary, gained in virulence primarily because of events in Fiume. The Fiume issue was not resolved at Paris, and the town pursued a quasi-autonomous existence until September 1919. At this point, the archnationalist romantic poet and renowned amorist, D'Annunzio, at the head of a legion of war veterans, seized Fiume "in the name of the Italian people." This illegal coup was greeted with acclaim in Italy, both by the superpatriots and by many establishment figures who normally upheld law and order. Yugoslavia did not move to expel D'Annunzio out of fear of the Italian government, while the authorities in Rome did not dare to act from fear of Italian popular sentiment. Indeed, the Nitti and Giolitti ministries covertly sent supplies to D'Annunzio. His seriocomic, self-styled regency survived until the end of 1920. Only then did the Giolitti government, having reached a frontier settlement with Yugoslavia which provided for an independent state of Fiume, find the will to send warships against D'Annunzio. Even so, it remains unclear whether Italian shells or an influenza epidemic was the major cause of the legionnaires' departure. D'Annunzio not only kept nationalist grievances in the forefront of Italy's consciousness; he also succeeded in exposing the futility of the parliamentary regime's foreign policy. Unable to satisfy Italian patriotism by imitating D'Annunzio, it was also incapable of curbing nationalist excesses.

Feebleness in domestic and foreign affairs left a power vacuum at the heart of Italian politics that gave Mussolini his opportunity. The twin myths of a bolshevik danger and a "mutilated victory" pushed Italy into the embrace of Fascism.

Fascism was formally inaugurated on March 23, 1919, in Milan's Piazza San Sepolcro; later, it would be a matter of Fascist pride to be a *sansepolcrista* or member of the first *fascio di combattimento*. (By now the word *fascio*, from the Latin *fasces* denoting the bundle of rods with protruding ax head carried by the magistrates of ancient Rome, was used in Italy for any political group, especially on the Right; Mussolini and others had adopted the word for their interventionist groups during the war.) Mussolini made two speeches at the founding of his new movement. In the morning, he struck the nationalist note. Claim was laid to Fiume, Dalmatia, and colonies; war veterans were eulogized and their shabby treatment censured. This was only appropriate, for a substantial part of the audience of about one hundred consisted of *arditi*—the shock troops of the Italian army known for bravery, brutality, and patriotic zeal. They were the prototype of all those Italian soldiers who could not adjust to civilian life because their values remained those of the battlefield. From them, the scorn for peaceful pursuits was passed on to many an Italian youth too young to have had first-hand experience of the excitement of war. It was from such ex- and would-be *arditi* that Mussolini constructed his paramilitary organization. The black uniform of the *arditi* became the blackshirt of the Fascists, the aim of both a rebirth of the militant nationalism of 1915–1918.

In the afternoon of March 23, Mussolini explained Fascism's social policy. Its main tenets were decidedly, and, in view of how Fascism would develop, surprisingly radical—antimonarchical, anticlerical, and anticapitalist. At this time, Mussolini had aspirations to be the Lenin of Italy. But besides attacking the established pillars of Italian society, Mussolini also struck out at the Socialist establishment. The P.S.I. he dismissed as "obviously reactionary, completely conservative." The brand of socialism Mussolini now espoused bore a strong imprint of syndicalism. Under the slogan of "economic democracy," he advocated worker control of industry, "because we want the workers to become accustomed to managerial responsibilities." Political representation should be, not by geography, but by "occupational outlook." Mussolini conceded that "such a program implies a return to the guilds (*corporazioni*)." Thus, Fascism proposed to make over syndicalist socialism into the corporative state.

Such was "urban fascism," proclaimed in Italy's industrial heartland and responsive to proletarian interests. Mussolini may have uttered these left-wing sentiments with complete sincerity. De Felice in *Mussolini: il rivoluzionario, 1883–1920* (1965) is inclined to accept his remarks at face value. In practice, however, they turned out to be little more than a gambit to win popular support. From the first moment, Fascist expenses for uniforms, arms, transport, as well as the continued publication of *Popolo d'Italia*, were met primarily by men of property. Of course, the gulf between the forces of capitalism and an ostensibly socialist movement should have been enormous. Without doubt, the capitalist camp showed unusual acumen in perceiving as early as 1919–1920 that Mussolini could be bought. For his part, Mussolini was so desperate for funds as to be patently opportunistic; he intended to use the capitalists as they did him.

At first, Mussolini's affiliation with the nationalist Right seems to have provided a bridge to capitalism; for example, the hall in the Piazza San Sepolcro where the first *fascio* met belonged to the Association of Commerce, Industry, and Agriculture, and was often leased to patriotic groups. But it was the furious escalation of the class war that consolidated the partnership between Fascism and property. First and foremost in this process was the employment during the winter of 1920 of Fascist paramilitary brawlers (*squadristi*) by the big landowners of Emilia and the Po Valley who were determined to break the newly won power of the peasant leagues and cooperatives. The significance of this "agrarian fascism" cannot be emphasized too much. Adrian Lyttleton in *Seizure of Power: Fascism in Italy, 1919–1929* (1973) observes that "agrarian fascism" differed markedly from the "urban fascism" of 1919; simply, it was unmistakably more terroristic and antidemocratic. While helping to make the Fascist movement into a national one, "agrarian fascism" also served to transform it irrevocably into a servant of the brutal Right. The year 1920 saw, too, the establishment of a General Confederation of Industry (*Confindustria*) whose avowed purpose was to counter working-class agitation by force if necessary. The *Confindustria* joined the landowners in swelling the Fascist treasury.

This coalition of Fascism and wealth was not, however, an unrelievedly reactionary plot. In *Agrarian Elites and Italian Fascism* (1982). A. Cardoza demonstrates that the northern landowners who backed Mussolini were not the old paternalistic aristocracy so much as a new commercial farming class. Since the turn of the century these entrepreneurs had shown no compunction in riding roughshod over the peasantry in a ruthless pursuit of profits and agrarian efficiency. In the same vein, many Italian industrialists subscribed to the post–First World War vogue of Taylorism or economic rationalism, and were willing to break heads for the sake of national modernization. Mussolini was quite prepared to pander to this hankering after technocratic advance, injecting into his speeches the slogan *"largo alle competenze"* (make way for the skillful). Thus Fascism and its propertied allies exhibited a progressive side. None the less, Italy's capitalists expected Fascism to speed up modernization by authoritarian means and a violent suppression of the Left.

Responding to their paymasters, the *squadristi* made a regular weekend sport out of raids on the offices of left-wing newspapers, rural cooperatives, and trade unions; sometimes the headquarters of white or Catholic unions were hit. Individuals deemed anti-Fascist were treated to a purging dose of castor oil or a beating with *bastone* or *manganello*, clubs favored by the *squadristi*. These expeditions were led by local Fascist bosses called *ras* after Ethiopian tribal chiefs. Many a future Fascist hierarch began as a *ras*—Dino Grandi in Bologna, Roberto Farinacci in Cremona, Italo Balbo in Ferrara. That such men operated independently was demonstrated by a curious episode in August 1921. Presumably in an attempt to recapture the image of original Fascism as a workers' movement, Mussolini concluded a pact with the Socialists for the renunciation of violence. He was immediately disavowed by a group of the *ras*, whereupon he resigned as Fascist leader. Within a few weeks, the quarrel was patched up and Mussolini returned as Duce, a generic title he had always cultivated both as Socialist and Fascist. His charismatic prowess was sufficiently clear by 1921 that the Fascist movement could ill afford to lose it. On the other hand, on the substantive issue Mussolini capitulated. Although the pact with the Socialists was not repudiated, the *ras* were assured that they need not abide by it. The affair suggested that Fascism might be taking on an existence of its own, independent of Mussolini.

The extent to which the Duce had given in to the antisocialist proclivities of his followers was evident at a Fascist congress in Rome in November. In the course of transforming Fascism from a movement into a party, the *Partito nazionale fascista* (P.N.F.), Mussolini redefined the Fascist program. Now Fascists were to be "decidedly antisocialist" and "economic liberals." As for the masses: "We do indeed wish to serve them, to educate them, but we also intend to flog them when they make mistakes." The *squadristi* hardly needed this encouragement. Italy was plunged into a veritable civil war between Fascist blackshirts and Socialist redshirts. Undoubtedly, there were provocations on both sides, but there is no question that the greater aggression came from the blackshirts. The deliberate stimulation of anarchy served to keep propertied interests in a state of alarm. With the government unable or unwilling to intervene, Fascism seemed the only safeguard; in effect, it acquired a monopoly of antibolshevism.

Fascism also cornered the nationalist market, somewhat surprisingly in view of D'Annunzio's apparent stranglehold on patriotism. To many D'Annunzio was a *duce;* in 1919 and 1920 he, not Mussolini, was touted as the likeliest leader of a coup against the liberal regime. Mussolini was perfectly aware that D'Annunzio was his potential rival; hence, his ambivalent attitude to D'Annunzio's seizure of Fiume. On the surface, Mussolini was deferential to the hero whom he described in *Popolo d'Italia* as "the Intrepid One." He visited Fiume for twenty-four hours, and at home solicited funds for D'Annunzio's illegal regency. On the other hand, a good deal of the money collected went into the Fascist coffers. More than once, D'Annunzio wrote privately to Mussolini, bitterly reproaching him for his lack of practical aid. Nor was Mussolini's moral support any more reliable. When the government in Rome signed the Treaty of Rapallo with Yugoslavia giving autonomy to Fiume, Mussolini failed to second D'Annunzio's immediate condemnation. Not until criticism of Rapallo became widespread in Italy did *Popolo d'Italia* come out circumspectly against the treaty. Shortly afterwards, on D'Annunzio's expulsion from Fiume, *Popolo d'Italia* expressed its regret with unmistakable reserve: "We must be thankful," Mussolini editorialized, "that the tragedy has not turned into a catastrophe."

In brief, Mussolini refused to commit himself to D'Annunzio. Rather, he preferred to learn from him. Much of what was later called the "*stile fascista*" (Fascist style) was conceived in direct imitation of D'Annunzio's Fiume adventure: the same posturing and martial swagger; similar uniforms and insignia; the equivalent leader's speech from the balcony to the crowd in the piazza below; the identical rhythmic war cries, comprehensible and otherwise ("For whom Italy? For whom the future? For us! Eja, Eja, Alalà!"). Even the corporative state D'Annunzio sketched at Fiume was to be imitated.

While gaining notoriety in Fiume, D'Annunzio lost ground in Italy. After the Fiume escapade was over, he had no political program or future. His social ideas were always too radical to permit him to embrace antibolshevism as Mussolini did. And Mussolini, who had corresponded with D'Annunzio about a joint march on Rome in 1921, refused to consider any such project when D'Annunzio returned to Italy. Meanwhile, the unemployed legionnaires from Fiume enrolled in the Fascist *squadre*. At the moment that the Fascists made their bid for power in 1922, D'Annunzio was conveniently put *hors de combat* by a head injury sustained in a mysterious fall from his balcony, for which, gossip suggested, the *squadristi* supplied the impetus. At all events, the nationalist hero swiftly and startlingly became, as one biographer calls him, "a lost leader," the cause of his eclipse still a matter of some conjecture. Mussolini, for his part, did what he could to hasten it and to profit by it. Amid the disappointment following D'Annunzio's retreat from Fiume, Fascist pronouncements on international affairs took on a new degree of strident chauvinism. It was a patent effort to hearten the nationalist cause, and it was gratefully received. During 1921, the Nationalist and Fascist parties began to work in ever-increasing unison, a process that was to culminate two years later in the actual fusion of the parties. Mussolini's appropriation of the nationalist leadership was of huge benefit in making Fascism acceptable in the respectable strata of Italian society. The Fascist Duce became the mentor of those whom the historian Federico Chabod, in his *History of Italian Fascism* (1963), terms "the educated *bourgeoisie,* people who read D'Annunzio and recalled the patriotic poet Carducci, and looked on the Risorgimento and the unification of Italy as the outstanding achievement of their forefathers."

By 1922, there was hardly any segment of the Italian establishment not ready to collaborate with Fascism either for nationalist or antibolshevik reasons, or both. At the very top of the social hierarchy, aristocratic nationalists provided an entree for Fascism into court circles. Mussolini helped by making another of his famous switches; in September 1922, he declared himself a monarchist. The queen mother, Margherita, who had been active in the rightist reaction of 1898, was an avid pro-Fascist. The king's cousin, the Duke d'Aosta, was sympathetic because he hoped that the Fascists planned a palace revolution which would put him on the throne. The king himself, Victor Emmanuel III, anticipated the same thing and remained complaisant to the Fascists to avert it.

The Vatican's benevolence was no less discernible. It was well known that Mussolini and Pius XI, who was elected pope in February 1922, were on cordial terms; the latter, when Archbishop of Milan, had allowed Fascist banners to be displayed in the Duomo. The official Vatican journal, *Osservatore Romano,* deplored the civil war between reds and blacks. But when it came to castigating specific acts of violence, socialist outrages were almost always cited. The Catholic faithful could and did draw the intended conclusion— that of the twin evils of socialism and Fascism, the latter was considered the lesser by a wide margin.

In like fashion and out of the same terror of bolshevism, the secular liberal papers by and large turned a blind eye to Fascist atrocities. Many of these journals had stood firm for civil liberties in the crisis of 1898–1900. Yet now, with Milan's enormously influential *Corriere della Sera* in the vanguard, Fascism's assault on the most elementary legal rights was justified as the only alternative to anarchy. A further rationalization was that Fascism would grow tamer with time; above all, it was claimed that tenure of office would breed a sense of responsibility. This argument was very strongly held in the upper echelons of the Italian bureaucracy, especially in the aristocratic and prestigious Foreign Ministry. The senior civil servants possessed a sublime confidence in their own ability to keep Mussolini, once in office, in check.

The hypothesis that Fascism could be made law-abiding provided comfort also to numerous Italian intellectuals who declined to take a clear stand against the movement. Indeed, the acquiescence of much of the intellectual community represented perhaps Mussolini's crowning success in ingratiating himself with all shades of opinion in the Italian power spectrum. It was not surprising that a scholar like Gaetano Mosca, who was in all his writings skeptical of parliamentary democracy, should find some value in Fascism. A more symbolic figure was Benedetto Croce, both because of his intellectual standing and because of the reverence for the liberal Italy born in 1861 displayed in his historical works. But Croce was a nationalist too, and his thought contained the seeds of that philosophy of action which Mussolini was trying to implement. In a series of press interviews, Croce communicated his conviction that Fascism was necessary and compatible with liberal principles, and as Croce decided, so did a great many of the Italian intelligentsia. In Italy, as elsewhere, "the betrayal of the intellectuals," to use Julien Benda's famous phrase, preceded the death of liberal politics.

Italian Fascism was a reaction against parliamentary democracy, and it made its way into office by the cultivation of influence mainly outside the Chamber of Deputies. Therefore, the Fascist performance in vote-catching and in parliamentary maneuvering could be of only peripheral concern. This is why the fiasco in the elections of 1919, in which the Fascists polled under 5,000 votes out of 270,000 in Milan, constituted no more than a temporary setback. Those socialists who paraded in front of Mussolini's home with a mock coffin bearing his name misread the situation and tempted fate. The elections of 1921 were run by Giolitti, who determined to transform the Fascists in the manner that he had transformed the reformist Socialists a generation ago. To bring the Fascists into Giolitti's parliamentary coalition, it was first necessary to include them in the national list of government-backed candidates. In consequence, Mussolini and thirty-four other Fascists were elected. This victory was a mark of how far Fascism had come in two years, and it conferred status on a movement anxious to impress the power structure with its seriousness. On the other hand, the Fascists refused to be transformed and took their seats with the Nationalists on the extreme right of the Chamber in opposition to Giolitti. Moreover, a parliamentary place did not deflect Fascism in the slightest from the use of force in the country at large, and the drive for power continued primarily by extraparliamentary means.

Despite its preference for power groups over parliamentary majorities, Fascism was not entirely without mass support. It never won the broad following of the Socialists or the *Popolari,* and few workers held high positions in the Fascist hierarchy. Nevertheless, the Fascist membership in 1921 was estimated at some 250,000. The bulk of Fascism's popular support came from the petty bourgeoisie or lower middle class, composed for the most part of small shopkeepers, clerical workers, and artisans, who although not the poor, were not so economically secure as to escape harm in the postwar slump. In addition, however, Italy's lower middle class included a sizable "intermediate elite" of teachers, journalists, and other "organic intellectuals" whose surfeit of high school and university diplomas availed nothing against a chronic shortage of appropriate white-collar jobs. But just as important as any material loss was the psychological impact of the alleged danger of bolshevism, for bolshevik egalitarianism threatened the social distinctions which elevated these segments of society above the proletariat. The lower middle class was caught between two giant forces, big business of which it was envious and labor of which it was fearful; it was not only the economic elite of *latifondisti* and factory owners who perceived a crisis of capitalism. Throughout Europe in the interwar years, whenever the lower middle class displayed a collective sense of insecurity, it tended to turn for protection to radical elements outside the traditional Right and traditional Left. Thus, Fascism gained a popular base by representing what the sociologist Seymour Lipset has called "an extremism of the center." Mussolini unerringly exploited the lower-middle-class neurosis. He could and did play the antibolshevik card to the utmost without incurring the odium of a conventional capitalist spokesman. More than one writer has summed up Mussolini as a petty bourgeois hero.

Had Fascism sought power by a grass-roots revolution, this

would have had to come from the lower middle class. Herein lay the only source of positive support for Fascism. But when all is said and done, Fascism triumphed through connivance with the aristocracy and upper bourgeoisie. These quarters provided negative support, in the sense that they tolerated Fascism so long as it performed certain tasks for them. It was a dangerous game to play. No one could be sure that Fascism might not prove to be a Frankenstein's monster, capable of turning on its master.

3

Power in Two Stages

The more the Fascists enjoyed the confidence of the power structure, the less they needed a violent coup to obtain power. And although, ostensibly, Fascism was swept into office by a march on Rome in October 1922, the importance of this paramilitary operation was much embellished after the fact. Eager to create the impression of Fascism as a revolutionary and vigorous movement, Fascist propaganda later asserted that power was taken by force in 1922. The truth is somewhat different.

Violence there certainly was. By the summer of 1922, the *squadristi* were strong enough to capture and hold the center of large towns for several days at a time. In such towns as Ferrara, Ravenna, and Parma it was made plain that both the elected town council and the local prefect appointed by Rome were subservient to Fascist authority. The same was true in Trieste where the Fascists used the pretext of protecting and encouraging Italian nationalism in the nation's newly acquired territory. In the Alto Adige, claiming similar justification, Fascism seized control of the entire regional administration. In the face of all this, the government remained supine; only in Bologna did a prefect on his own initiative stand up to the Fascists. But the Socialists, who saw themselves driven from their positions of strength in town councils won at the polls, determined on one final counterattack. On August 1, a general strike was launched. It backfired dismally. The workers' response was tepid, and the strike was called off after twenty-four hours—"the Caporetto of Italian socialism" was an apt contemporary metaphor.

The strike was a godsend to Mussolini; at a crucial moment it served to refurbish his claim to stand as "a dike against the red flood." It provided an excuse for further Fascist lawlessness. On August 3, the *squadristi* invaded the city hall of Milan and expelled its Socialist administration. Milan was Italy's richest city, the home of both Italian socialism and Fascism, and the real capital of Italy. Obviously, it was only a matter of time before an attack on the legal capital, Rome. On October 24, addressing a huge Fascist rally in Naples, Mussolini issued the call: "Either they will give us the government or we shall seize it by descending on Rome: it is now a matter of days, perhaps hours."

The March on Rome was entrusted to a quadrumvirate, which interestingly reflected the diverse elements within Fascism. General Emilio De Bono, the eldest, was a retired army officer and a nationalist of the old school; Italo Balbo, the youngest and typical of the extremist wing of Fascism, had acquired his taste for violence and chauvinism in the war; Cesare De Vecchi was from the ultraconservative landowning class and a staunch monarchist; Michele Bianchi, secretary of the Fascist party, had reached Fascism, like Mussolini himself, by the syndicalist socialist route. The quadrumvirate had at their disposal a regular Fascist militia (actually the *squadristi* put under military regulations in early October.) This force was to perform two operations: first, the capture of key provincial post and telegraph offices, police stations, railroad junctions, and the like in order to cut off the government in Rome from the rest of Italy; second, a simultaneous advance on Rome from different directions by three Fascist columns. Perugia was chosen as the headquarters of the quadrumvirate and the morning of October 28 as the moment for the coup to unfold. But it takes two to fight; if the Fascists were ready to throw down a challenge, it was not at all certain that the liberal regime in Rome would take it up.

Although the quadrumvirate kept secret their exact plans, rumors of a Fascist coup were rife throughout the fall of 1922. In this situation, the professional politicians all along showed that their preference was to ward off the threat by bringing the Fascists into the government itself. The archtransformist, Giolitti, was now an octogenarian but still eager to form one more ministry. At times of crisis, Giolitti customarily avoided the limelight, so now he remained at his home in Piedmont and used the pro-Fascist prefect of Milan as intermediary with Mussolini. Giolitti tried to strike a bargain out of disagreeable necessity; other politicians in Rome of a conservative stamp were more visibly enthusiastic for a coalition with the Fascists. Their prototype was the ex-wartime premier, Antonio Salandra, whose chief Fascist contact was with the aristocratic De Vecchi. Furthermore, the current premier, Luigi Facta, was well aware that his ministry was a stopgap arrangement and likely to fall at any moment. His preoccupation during October was to recast and strengthen it by incorporating the Fascists. Of course, Giolitti, Salandra, and Facta all planned that the Fascists would be a junior partner in a new coalition. The Fascist recourse to a *coup d'état* announced that this was not enough; the Fascists clearly expected the upper hand in any government that they joined. The March on Rome, then, was not planned to bring Fascism into office, but to ensure that it would enter office at the top level.

Inexcusably, the Facta ministry was taken by surprise at the first signs of Fascist mobilization on October 26. A proclamation of martial law was the obvious stratagem to protect Rome, but the king's signature was needed for this and he was on vacation near Pisa. Victor Emmanuel returned to Rome on the evening of the 27th and agreed to sign a proclamation if his ministers asked him to the next morning. At this, Facta and his colleagues, who had been thinking mostly of resignation, took heart. They determined to fight, and overnight placards announcing imminent martial law were affixed to the walls of Rome. The government had at hand more than sufficient military strength to disperse the 17,000 or so *squadristi* preparing to descend on Rome; these were equipped to provoke civil disturbances, not to conduct a full-scale military campaign. The question was whether the army, large portions of which were undeniably pro-Fascist, would do its duty. Both the chief of staff, General Badoglio, and General Pugliese, the military commandant of Rome, were convinced that the army would remain loyal to the king. On the whole, the chances of the liberal regime emerging victorious from a showdown of force with the Fascists were bright, but everything depended on the authorities in Rome keeping their nerve.

In fact, nerves did break. On the morning of the 28th, the king refused to sign the proclamation of martial law. No definitive explanation of this *volte-face* has been established. It has usually been assumed that overnight Victor Emmanuel was subject to various sorts of pressure—from Salandra's friends eager to undermine the Facta ministry, and from Fascist sympathizers at court who seem to have fed the king deliberately exaggerated figures of Fascist mobilization. On the other hand, several memorialists have implied that Facta had more to do with the matter than he ever admitted. Facta, a lawyer by profession, was known to be an ineffectual politician. The witticism of the day went that he should have been called Verba because he talked but did not act. It is not incredible that Facta panicked at the last minute and communicated his panic to the king, who thereupon declined to back up his vacillating ministers. But whoever was responsible, to forswear martial law was to leave the liberal regime defenseless. The Fascists would now either seize power or be given it on their own terms.

Mussolini saw this more clearly than any of the other protagonists in the drama. He was awaiting events in Milan, which was explicable insofar as Milan was the home of Fascism. It was also, as some unkindly pointed out, close to the Swiss frontier in case things went wrong. Certainly, of the Fascist leaders Mussolini was one of the most circumspect. It had been at his behest that the blackshirts marching on Rome were under strict orders to avoid clashes with army units. (The order was, of course, unknown to the government side.) So anxious was Mussolini to avoid a test of physical strength that on October 27 he had seemed on the verge of accepting a secondary place in a Giolittian ministry. Bianchi, in Rome, had thought it wise more than once to phone Milan in order to stiffen Mussolini's resolve against this temptation. But at the news of the martial law fiasco, Mussolini's irresolution vanished completely. During the 28th, Salandra, on behalf of the king, made a last-ditch effort to inveigle Mussolini into a coaliltion dominated by non-Fascist conservatives and nationalists. Although Salandra managed to enlist De Vecchi and Grandi in this enterprise, Mussolini flatly refused to consider the idea. His terms were unconditional: carte blanche to form his own government. With the Fascist columns now mobilized some forty miles from Rome, the king and his advisers were no longer able to quibble. In any case, Fascism was scarcely anathema to them. Victor Emmanuel was anything but dismayed when, about midday on the 29th, he asked De Vecchi to phone Mussolini and convey an invitation to come to Rome to form whatever ministry he saw fit. Cautious to the end, Mussolini insisted on receiving the summons in writing. On the evening of the 29th, the appropriate telegram arrived in Milan, at which the Duce departed for Rome by railway sleeping car.

Mussolini became premier on October 30—before any of his *squadristi* reached Rome. Outwardly, then, the transfer of power took place acording to constitutional form. It could hardly be called a *coup d'état* because the authorities surrendered before a blow could be struck. Some of the headstrong *ras* felt cheated at the short-circuiting of their adventure. To placate them, a day later the blackshirts were brought by special train to Rome; there they paraded in rather bedraggled condition—for they had been sitting in the autumn rain for forty-eight hours—before Mussolini and the king. On the other hand, the pacific outcome of the March on Rome suited Mussolini's taste. As a cautious politico, he had been pushed into the background during the military preparations for the march, but by grasping the opportunity offered by the cancellation of martial law, he was catapulted once more into the forefront of Fascist councils. Shrewder than the blackshirt hotheads, he recognized that Fascism's success rested, not on its own strength, but on the ineptitude of its opponents. Out of this diagnosis sprang the spirit of compromise which infused the early actions of Fascism in power.

The cabinet that Mussolini constructed within twelve hours of his arrival in Rome contained fourteen members, of which only four were actually Fascists. The key posts naturally went to these Fascists; Mussolini himself became president of the Council of Ministers, pro tem foreign minister, and minister of the interior. None the less, the presence of Nationalists, *Popolari*, and even two reformist socialists, made this appear a conventional transformist ministry. Also in traditional style, the ministry requested a vote of confidence in parliament. True, Mussolini threw out the Cromwellian hint that he would cheerfully get along without parliament if it tried to cross him. But at the time, this tended to be dismissed as an academic threat, for the new government received the backing of the parliamentary magnates and erstwhile premiers—such as Giolitti, Salandra, Orlando, and Bonomi. With only the left-wing parties voting negatively in bulk, Mussolini's government won handsome majorities in the Chamber of Deputies and the Senate. Furthermore, parliament was induced to allow the cabinet extraordinary powers for one year. This was not unique; the right to govern by decree for a limited time had been frequently granted in the past half-century. It was a little unusual this time in that the government could not describe the policies which its executive power would implement. "Before achieving this position," declaimed Mussolini on his first appearance before parliament as premier, "we were asked on all sides for a program. It is not programs, alas, which are lacking in Italy: only the men and the will to apply programs. . . . This will, firm and decisive, is represented by the government today." However, all that seemed to matter was that things were being done within a legal framework.

Mussolini's personal demeanor was carefully modulated to dispel suspicion that he was an incipient dictator. As constitutional precedent dictated, he reported regularly to the king—twice a week, in fact, on Monday and Thursday mornings. On these occasions and in many public appearances, he discarded his Fascist blackshirt for a conventional statesman's dress—wing collar, cutaway coat, even spats. He looked obviously uncomfortable in this attire, and awkward at social ceremonies which as premier he was expected to attend. So he submitted to lessons in deportment and protocol at the hands of his foreign ministry staff. He was equally willing at first to learn the paperwork of his job. *"Un ottimo funzionario"* (a superior bureaucrat), observed one career diplomat approvingly.

Not surprisingly, all this tractability did not sit well with the *ras*. Their ambition was to overthrow the old order as soon as possible and preferably by direct action; in the P.N.F. language of the day they demanded that a "second wave" of Fascism follow on the acquisition of political power. The struggle between this fanatic ardor and Mussolini's tactical moderation kept the Fascist movement in a state of tension for two years. One device that Mussolini conceived to advance his views was a permanent assembly of a score or so Fascist chiefs. This Grand Council of Fascism, created in December 1922, enabled Mussolini to keep under scrutiny his most powerful rivals. More important, it imposed a hierarchical structure on Fascism with Mussolini at the apex. The Duce chose the members of the Grand Council; he served as its permanent president; and he alone triggered its decision-making process. Almost the first action of the Grand Council was to convert the *squadristi* into a national militia financed by the state—*Milizia volontaria per la sicurezza nazionale* (M.V.S.N.). This was represented as another token of Fascism's renunciation of extralegal methods. Actually, all members of the M.V.S.N. swore allegiance, not to the king, but to the Duce; thus, a private army was institutionalized and brought under Mussolini's personal control. To assert authority on paper was one thing; it was another in practice. To a considerable extent, the provincial *ras* called the tune in their own bailiwicks, and indulged in sporadic violence contrary to the image of respectability that Mussolini induced in Rome.

It was not that Mussolini was opposed to the use of violence itself; far from it, and several recent studies have detailed acts of gratuitous cruelty (in Italy's colonial empire, for example.) In 1922, it was rather that Mussolini preferred to employ violence selectively as part of a broader scheme. He was concerned to keep alive an ambience of turmoil and intimidation against which he could move to consolidate his power by legal means—the same strategy, in fact, that had succeeded so well in the March on Rome. Mussolini was no less determined than the *ras* to augment Fascist power; for Machiavellian reasons he chose to preserve a veneer of legality as long as possible.

Parliament's backing of his ministry seemed sound enough at first, but then in Italian parliamentary history majorities were apt to vanish with remarkable swiftness. The Fascists possessed only 35 seats out of 535 in the Chamber of Deputies. Even the formal amalgamation with the Nationalists in February 1923 added only 10 seats. In the spring of 1923, a rift opened between Mussolini and the *Popolari*, many of whom were distressed by continued Fascist brutality in the countryside. The upshot was that Mussolini dismissed the Popular ministers from his cabinet. The Popular party's reaction was muted, as indicated by the announcement that, while it could no longer support Mussolini's government, neither would it join the opposition. Nevertheless, the episode illustrated how fragile was the parliamentary coalition that supplied a constitutional basis for Fascist rule. At this point, Mussolini brought forward the Acerbo election law.

This piece of legislation, named after the Fascist deputy who introduced it into parliament, repealed the law of 1919 on proportional representation, which had been designed to thwart parliamentary dictatorship. It provided that the party gaining the most votes in a national election (so long as it received at least one quarter of the total) should automatically be given two thirds of the seats in the Chamber of Deputies. It was a patent attempt to overcome the chronic instability of postwar Italian governments—in itself a worthwhile endeavor. Suspicion attached to it mostly because the motives of the Fascists in proposing it were suspect, but after heated debate in both chambers of parliament, the bill became law by the end of 1923.

Elections were held the following April. Although to his fellow

Fascists Mussolini might profess scorn for election returns, the Acerbo Law indicated that he would brook no defeat. He followed the standard practice of submitting a government-approved list of candidates drawn from diverse political groups; in this case, Fascists and non-Fascists were included. A wide range of candidates was calculated to afford the government the maximum chance of a majority. But not content with this time-honored ploy, Mussolini gave his lieutenants free rein to use force to ensure an election victory. Violence was far from unknown in pre-Fascist Italian elections, but April 1924 witnessed a new level of systematic terror. This was anything but a free election. The remarkable thing is that as many as two and a half million voted against the government. On the other hand, either voluntarily or under threat, 65 percent of the votes were cast for Mussolini's list. His parliamentary position was secured—without reliance on the Acerbo system of allotting seats. Mussolini's policy of remaining, nominally at least, within the framework of the constitution had paid another dividend. Yet ironically in this moment of victory, the epilogue of the election impelled Mussolini into a blatantly illegal course of the sort that he had skillfully avoided hitherto.

Fascist terror tactics in the election did not go unprotested. Most articulate of the protesters was a prominent socialist, Giacomo Matteotti, whose remarks sparked fisticuffs in the Chamber of Deputies and a Mussolinian threat to put his opponents before a firing squad. To his friends, Matteotti confided that he feared for his life. In the afternoon of June 10, Matteotti was attacked on the sidewalk outside his home by five men who bundled him into a car which sped off. Through the windows a melee of flying arms was seen by at least two witnesses who alertly took the car's number. As a result, the police quickly found the car, which proved to have a blood-stained interior, and arrested five Fascist ex-*arditi*. The ringleader was one, Amerigo Dumini, who served as assistant to Cesare Rossi, head of Mussolini's press bureau. It was not until August that Matteotti's body with knife wounds was discovered in a shallow grave in the country north of Rome. But long before this, all Italy was sure that Matteotti had been killed by Fascists, and had assumed that Mussolini was implicated.

The murder was indeed the work of the Dumini gang who confessed to it. About Mussolini's exact part there is room for debate, although of his moral guilt there is no question. We know that he was in the habit of sending out instructions "to make life difficult" for specific enemies of the government. (The phrase was used in a telegram to the Fascist prefect of Turin who was to apply it to a young anti-Fascist journalist, Piero Gobetti. Gobetti was beaten up and fled to France, where he died of his injuries at the age of twenty-four.) From the judicial investigation of the Matteotti affair, conducted secretly at the time, we now know that a special strong-arm squad had recently been formed under Dumini, with an office in Mussolini's own Ministry of the Interior. Its express task was to terrorize anti-Fascist spokesmen into silence. By order from the top, Matteotti was singled out as a prime target. "That man should not be permitted to walk around," Mussolini is reported to have commented to Rossi. It is noteworthy that Rossi and Dumini occupied posts which kept them close to the Duce; they could reasonably claim to know his mind. Yet, no specific Mussolinian order to kill Matteotti has ever come to light. Predictably, there are those who would absolve the Duce of blame, but the consensus of scholarly opinion is surely justified in insisting on Mussolini's ultimate responsibility.

It is said that Henry II of England once asked rhetorically: "Who will rid me of this turbulent priest?" And the murder of Thomas Becket followed. Henry did not explicitly order Becket's assassination, nor perhaps did Mussolini command that Matteotti be killed outright. The crimes were similar. Each ruler instigated an assault on an enemy and must be held accountable when the violence got out of hand.

Whether Dumini and his associates set out to commit premeditated murder is arguable. The killing itself was done in a fumbling, apparently improvised manner. On the other hand, it may be that certain Fascists had a motive for exaggerating Mussolini's injunction to deal with Matteotti. One somewhat unorthodox interpretation is that Matteotti's murder was an antisocialist plot. In founding the Fascist movement, Mussolini had aspired to integrate all Italians into a Fascist state, not to perpetuate the class war. More than once, he had tried to build a bridge to the Left, and after his success in the elections of April 1924, he was in a strong position to resume the effort. Several of Mussolini's colleagues have testified that he was indeed contemplating a fresh overture. For the congenital antisocialists among the Fascists, what better way was there to prevent this than to kill an eminent socialist, ostensibly on Mussolini's orders? Mussolini himself gave some credence to this notion when, twenty years later, he referred to "the corpse that on June 10, 1924, was thrown between me and the socialists." Admittedly, Mussolini may well have been rationalizing after the event. But at any rate, in 1924 he gave the appearance, feigned or not, of being taken aback by the murder, and he was certainly unprepared for the storm it aroused.

Matteotti was not the first to die at Fascist hands, although he was the most prominent. It was mainly the timing of the crime that caused shock-waves to reverberate throughout Italy and indeed the world. Coming on top of the recent election violence and two years after Mussolini became premier, it made a mockery of the contention that Fascism would grow milder with the responsibilities of office. A sudden upsurge of public revulsion against Fascism spurred the parliamentary opposition into a symbolic demonstration. Under the leadership of the Liberal Giovanni Amendola, it repeated the stratagem that had defeated the Right in the crisis of 1898–1900. On June 27, a mixed group of Liberals, *Popolari*, and Socialists withdrew from parliament in an Aventine secession. Needless to say, this was merely a gesture; in effect, the Aventines waited for someone else to take positive action against Mussolini. In view of the king's crucial part in making Mussolini premier, many looked to Victor Emmanuel for guidance. But having made his choice in 1922, the king decided for safety's sake to stick with it. Most of the advice he received was to bide his time; such was the burden of Giolitti's and Salandra's counsel. Another hypothetical rallying-point against Fascism was the Vatican. But in September, Pope Pius XI warned the Popular party against joining an anti-Fascist front if it meant co-operation with atheistic socialism. The reluctant attitudes of king and pope summarized the problem in a nutshell: fearful of who or what might replace Mussolini, the entire Italian power structure was slow to admit that its creature, Fascism, was out of control. And without leadership from within the power structure, the anti-Fascist opposition remained fragmented and embryonic.

Despite this oppositional inefficacy, Mussolini showed every sign of panic. He oscillated between such defiance as a decree to permit press censorship and almost groveling appeals for sympathy. To exonerate himself, he offered scapegoats for Matteotti's murder. He forced the resignation of Rossi, who was Dumini's nominal superior. Because the Dumini gang had plainly operated with police collusion, he fired Aldo Finzi, the Fascist undersecretary of the Ministry of the Interior, and also General De Bono, the director of public security. In reality, the maneuver backfired; both Finzi and Rossi circulated memoranda implicating Mussolini in the crime. He seemed to avoid confronting the Chamber of Deputies, preferring votes of confidence in the highly conservative Senate. Yet without the Aventines, the Chamber was merely a rump assembly. When it finally met in November after a five-month hiatus, it gave Mussolini an overwhelming majority. Of course, Mussolini well knew that the true temper of the nation was to be discerned outside parliament. He set much store by the deserted aspect of the Palazzo Venezia, which he had made the seat of his administration, as the timeservers of his regime stayed away, awaiting developments. Occasional visitors found him alone in his office, often unshaven and red-eyed, in fear of a popular uprising. November was the nadir of his depression. The parliamentary mandarins, Giolitti and Orlando, came out in belated opposition to his government. Just as important, the *Corriere della Sera* grew more hostile with every issue. It may be that about this time Mussolini actually tendered his resignation, only to have it refused by Victor Emmanuel. Whether this was so or not, he certainly made it clear that, if requested by the king to resign, he would do so.

Mussolini's difficulties were compounded by the fact that his spasmodic attempts to appease the constitutionalists created trouble within his own party. From the outset one Fascist segment had wanted to use the Matteotti affair as an excuse to smash the opposition, break with legality and the establishment, and inaugurate a radical new order in Italy. Ultimately, it was these extremists who jolted Mussolini out of his paralysis. The climax came in December when Mussolini allowed Balbo to be forced out of his post as commander in chief of the militia; Balbo was a hero of the activists. The reaction was most bitter among the provincial bosses, the *ras* who now enjoyed the title of Fascist consuls. The revolt of the consuls, as it is sometimes called, aimed first at compelling Mussolini to reassert Fascism by a return to force; failing that, there remained the possibility of deposing the Duce. As a means of pressure on Mussolini, on December 31 a giant rally of Tuscan Fascists was held at Florence. There, loyalty to the Duce was declared to be conditional on his taking "dictatorial action." On the same day, a deputation of thirty consuls visited Mussolini in Rome on the pretext of conveying new year greetings; in truth, they came to expostulate at his deference to liberal sentiment. Four days earlier, the explosive Rossi memorandum had been published in Amendola's paper, undermining still further Mussolini's standing with the moderates and the respectable. It has been suggested that Mussolini was a party to the consuls' agitation in order to pave the way for strong action that he had already decided on. But this is doubtful. More likely, capitulation to the consuls seemed the line of least resistance, and he took it.

On January 3, 1925, Mussolini made a major policy address to the Chamber of Deputies. For the first time, he accepted the onus for Matteotti's death: "I declare before all Italy that I assume full responsibility for what has happened." He did not hide the fact that this disregard of moderate opinion presaged a dictatorship: "Italy wants peace and quiet, and calm in which to work. This we shall give her, by love if possible, by force if need be." And there proved to be nothing to stop Mussolini now. Over the past few years, there had been too much compromise by non-Fascists and too much hesitancy by anti-Fascists to mount resistance to this new coup. During 1925–1926, four assassination attempts were made on Mussolini's life, but none sprang from a deep-seated opposition movement. (Indeed, one was probably a charade staged by the government itself to justify extending the dictatorship.) Within these two years, Mussolini's ministry ceased to be a coalition and became exclusively Fascist. The Aventine secessionists, when they tried to return to parliament, were barred at the door by armed blackshirts; anti-Fascist parties were proscribed; and parliament, reduced to the proverbial rubber stamp, accorded Premier Mussolini a virtually limitless right to rule by decree. Local elections were stopped; the prefect and a new official named the *podestà*, both appointed in Rome, took over from elected mayors and councils. Independent trade unions, socialist and Catholic, were outlawed. Perhaps most important, however, was suppression of the free press. Independent newspapers, rather than a malleable parliament, had always been the true forum of Italian public opinion. Now not only was censorship imposed, but Fascist stooges were put in charge of such famous liberal papers as Milan's *Corriere della Sera* and Turin's *La Stampa*. By the end of 1926, which Mussolini liked to call his Napoleonic year, the foundations of the dictatorship had been securely laid. It has been well said that the Matteotti affair set in motion the conversion of a government into a regime.

4
In Power

Fascism achieved absolute power under Mussolini although not necessarily because of him. The extremists had often forced Mussolini's hand, and the resolution of the Matteotti crisis on their terms represented a supreme triumph. Paradoxically, it also marked the end of their influence. This was almost bound to happen. After January 3, 1925, there were no grounds for challenging Mussolini's leadership; by committing himself to a "second wave" of Fascism, Mussolini had apparently joined the extremists. This was illustrated by the appointment of Roberto Farinacci as party secretary, whose job it was to assert Mussolini's fiat in the party. Farinacci himself had been prominent in the revolt of the consuls, but once Mussolini came around to the consuls' view, Farinacci advocated a rigid party structure to further the revolution. Within two years the power of the independent *ras* was broken.

Now that parliament no longer mattered, the decrees by which Italy was governed emanated from the Grand Council of Fascism. The Grand Council, however, acted as no more than a rubber stamp for the wishes of its president who was, of course, the Duce. Meanwhile, Fascist propaganda, soon to blanket the whole country, presented Mussolini as the embodiment of Fascist virtue. It was impossible to polish his image without adding to his authority as well. Mussolini himself demanded that everything be kept under his thumb, and he usually held several ministries at once. Often, he busied himself with trivia—the date on which the Roman police should change into summer uniform, the names of civil servants not at their desks by 9 A.M., or scandal files he kept on innumerable Italians. Needless to say, more important matters were left unattended, in spite of the Palazzo Venezia lights blazing well into the night to create the illusion that the Duce never slept. Nevertheless, there was no denying the reality of his power. After January 3, 1925, Mussolini's unchallenged central role meant that Italian Fascism would now be what he made it.

The man who thus became the veritable dictator of his party and of his country was, in January 1925, forty-one years of age. Mussolini was below average height, five feet six inches, although very stockily built like his blacksmith father. Since his youth, he had been clean-shaven, and also since he was young, his hairline had receded rapidly; this threw into relief his sallow, round face whose main features were a jutting jaw, a large mobile mouth, and dark protuberant eyes. This less than impressive appearance he contrived to offset by his mannerisms. To disguise his short stature he always stood ramrod straight, pushed out his lower lip and jaw, and tilted back his head; thus, his eyes seemed to look down, never up, at a person. He loved to stand next to Victor Emmanuel at parades because he dwarfed the diminutive monarch. When he went into the countryside, he would stop to help in the fields, which gave him a chance to strip to the waist and exhibit his sturdy torso. He had a flair for costume; after 1925 he spurned civilian dress as much as possible and went back to uniforms in which he cut a figure of strength and authority.

Mussolini did not enjoy good health. Before the war, he had contracted syphilis, and many have suspected that this plagued him throughout his life. What, without question, he did suffer from perennially was a gastric ulcer. Indeed, the Napoleonic year, 1926, had to be interrupted by an operation. Because of his ulcer Mussolini always ate sparingly, rarely touching meat and drinking very little wine. Naturally, this human frailty had to be hidden from the world, for the Duce was supposed to epitomize virility. So the Fascist press pictured him as a sportsman: riding horses over jumps that appeared taller than they were because the camera was placed at ground level, driving fast cars and airplanes, and playing with a lion cub which someone gave him as a present.

In reality, his sole preoccupation was politics, and he had little taste for leisure recreations. He claimed to read a good deal in the classics, history, and political science, although the evidence indicates that he usually skimmed a book as briefly as possible to obtain its highlights. This enabled him to pepper his conversation with literary references. He did this most successfully in a famous series of interviews with the writer Emil Ludwig, who duly commented in his *Talks with Mussolini* (1933) on the Duce's breadth of reading. Mussolini's interest in art was minimal. For relaxation he would sometimes play the violin, but this was seldom publicized lest it be deemed effete by Fascist standards.

In his personal relationships, Mussolini was a complete egoist. He used others shamelessly, often inflicting pain out of a monumental insensitivity to anyone else's feelings. He bragged that friendship was alien to him, and was always ready to sacrifice his colleagues to save his own face. The pedestal on which the Duce stood at the apex of his regime discouraged familiarity, and one contemporary journalist was appalled at "his terrifying solitude and lack of contact with ordinary humankind." The only beings for whom he evinced anything like deep affection were his father and his brother, Arnaldo. He had a sentimental attachment to his children, especially to his second son, Bruno, and to his elder daughter, Edda. Yet, he was anything but a family man.

In 1910 Rachele Guido, the daughter of the woman who became his father's mistress after the death of Mussolini's mother, became his common-law wife; in 1916 they went through a civil marriage; and in 1925, when Mussolini saw fit to mute his anticlericalism, there was a religious ceremony. Rachele was a plain, honest country woman with no interest in politics; Mussolini hardly ever required her to attend receptions or to entertain. She bore him five children and looked after Mussolini as much as he allowed her to. She put up stoically with his neglect and his endless infidelities. Mussolini was openly proud of his sexual prowess in what a later generation would call a male chauvinist way. He was reputed never to be at a loss for a mistress, although he treated them all cavalierly. Rumor had it that his office was a favorite trysting place where he would seize his partner roughly, throw her to the floor, and make love to her there and then. Clara Petacci, who became his last mistress in 1936, received somewhat more respect than her predecessors. She was the young wife of an air force officer with a schoolgirl prettiness and manner. Mussolini found her gaiety a relief from the grim events of the last decade of his life, and she was rewarded with her own apartment in the Palazzo Venezia.

Mussolini boasted that he had most success with women and crowds. "The crowd loves strong men," he once said; "the crowd is like a woman." Gustave Le Bon's psychological study, *The Crowd* (1896), was apparently one work he took seriously to heart, and demagoguery came easily to him. Many of his traits that were disconcerting at close quarters—the facial contortions and the trick of rolling his eyes so that the whites showed—proved effective when viewed from the piazza below the celebrated balcony of the Palazzo Venezia, from which Mussolini liked to harangue the Romans. But, above all, his voice was his major asset. Trained in hundreds of street-corner speeches, it was at once powerful and flexible. The printed word cannot convey the essence of a Mussolinian speech. In content, it was a series of sharp, usually unconnected statements: "declamatory rather than persuasive," in the words of one English listener. The presentation was everything. All who heard him, friend and foe alike, have testified to his unerring ability to establish rapport with a crowd and to stimulate it. He possessed that mystic quality of leadership known as charisma.

Although he might move men to action, Mussolini himself shied away from it. Many of his close associates who observed his indecision during the March on Rome and the Matteotti affair, in speaking privately, used the word timid of Mussolini. It was not that he was devoid of physical courage; when wounded in one assassination attempt, he displayed remarkable coolness. But in a crisis his habit was to stand aside. He seemed to lack self-confidence, and it was noticed that he tended to follow the advice of whoever spoke to him last. The picture of the strong, resolute Duce that was sold to the world was the work of a superb public relations expert whose forte lay in words and images, not in deeds and actuality. Mussolini's onetime colleague, the socialist Giacinto Serrati, summed him up not too inaccurately when he wrote: "He is a rabbit; a phenomenal rabbit; he roars. Observers who do not know him mistake him for a lion."

Almost certainly Mussolini suffered from an outsized inferiority complex. His external self-assertiveness was doubtless a psychic compensation for his inner doubt. This personality trait seems to have been reflected in the policies which he imposed on Italy. Customarily, these sounded pretentious when announced but tended to be lethargically executed in the event. Like many crowd-pleasers, Mussolini proved to be better at criticizing existing faults than at implementing reform. Rather than following any blueprint for society, he seemed to make up his policies as he went along. In particular, he entered into a series of arrangements with the major interest groups of pre-Fascist Italy, with the result that the Mussolini government degenerated into a routine, albeit authoritarian, administration. This loss of Fascist momentum is conveyed in De Felice's celebrated distinction between *"fascismo-movimento"* and *"fascismo-regime"*—the former a radical and vibrant force descended in left-wing tradition from the French Revolution and dedicated to reshaping Italian society from top to bottom, the latter a conformist and opportunistic dictatorship preoccupied with the retention of power.

Symptomatic of the way in which an early promise of innovation yielded after 1925 to bureaucratic inertia was the fate of Italian Fascism's most authentic contribution to twentieth-century political theory—modern corporativism. The idea of a corporative state can be found in Mussolini's speeches right after the war, and the first Fascist corporations antedated the March on Rome. But the elaboration of a systematic theory ran afoul of the Fascist insistence that action itself was the highest virtue. The slogan "me ne frego" ("I don't give a damn") expressed the true Fascist's scorn for principles and intellectual self-justification. Consequently, the enunciation of corporative doctrine, to which Mussolini set his mind in the late 1920s, appeared an artificial veneer on an essentially unprincipled movement. It has always been suspected that Mussolini approached corporativism, less out of cerebral conviction, than out of the utilitarian calculation that Fascism lacked status without a political philosophy of its own.

The task of defining corporativism fell into several hands. Most influential was Alfredo Rocco, one of many Nationalists who found a home in Fascism. An authoritarian jurist, Rocco played a prominent role in drafting the repressive legislation of the dictatorship in 1925–1926. For a formal statement of the theory of corporativism, however, Mussolini turned to the philosopher, Giovanni Gentile, a prestigious recruit to Fascism and minister of education from 1922 to 1925. But Mussolini could not resist intervening and he arbitrarily revised Gentile's work. The joint efforts of Gentile and Mussolini produced an authoritative article on corporativism in volume XIV of the *Enciclopedia italiana* (1932). Corporativism was put forward as an alternative "third way" between capitalism and socialism, which were held to be divisive forces in modern society—the former because it sanctioned the pursuit of self-interest, the latter because it stimulated the class war. Before all else, corporativism was a device to restore social cohesion. To accomplish this, the economic activity of the nation was to be divided into categories, each represented by a corporation. Within the corporations, spokesmen for rival groups and classes would be brought face to face more directly than in traditional parliamentary institutions. It was also intended that the corporations would offer a more permanent and friendlier forum for negotiation than that in which trade union bargaining usually occurred. All parties would have every opportunity to perceive the common good, and harmony would ensue more or less spontaneously.

The corporative ideal was an old one that the Fascists updated.

The medieval guild, like the Fascist corporation, comprehended all classes within one vocation. The notion of society as a corporate unit was axiomatic in Christian Europe before the Reformation. This corporative heritage the modern Catholic church had recently summoned to its aid. Pope Leo XIII's famous encyclical of 1891, *De Rerum Novarum*, was a benign call for class collaboration in rebuttal of Marxian socialism; the message was repeated forty years later in the encyclical, *Quadragesimo Anno*. However, Mussolini's corporativism originated not in Christian teaching but in Sorelian syndicalism. He was in this respect typical of a generation of Italian petty bourgeois intellectuals who, disenchanted with Marxism, found a revolutionary surrogate in syndicalist ideas. From syndicalism derived the seminal notion that representation and authority in the modern state should rest on economic function. The syndicalists got their name from their emphasis on the French *syndicat* (in Italian *sindacato*, meaning trade union.) The Fascists echoed the emphasis on economic associations, but expanded the *sindacato* from a labor union into a corporation of both employers and employees.

The groundwork of the Fascist corporative state was laid in 1925 in the Vidoni Pact (it was signed in the Palazzo Vidoni.) By this the *Confindustria* and the Confederation of Fascist Trade Unions recognized each other as the legitimate representative of, respectively, capital and labor. The traditional trade unions were thus effectively neutralized. The following year, the Rocco Law, named for Rocco who was by now minister of justice, designated seven branches of economic activity—industry, agriculture, banking, commerce, internal transport, the merchant marine, and the intellectual community. Only in the last category was a genuine corporation established; in the other six, "syndical confederations" of property owners were distinct from worker confederations. However, notwithstanding the shortage of true corporations, a Ministry of Corporations was created in 1926; Giuseppe Bottai, another Fascist theoretician, was put in charge. In 1930, a National Council of Corporations drew together some delegates from capital- and labor-style confederations, but not until 1934 did the mixed corporations of employers and employees come into existence. There were twenty-two of them, as the older economic units were subdivided. Then, in 1938, the capstone was set on the corporate edifice. The Chamber of Deputies based on territorial representation was abolished. The next year, a Chamber of Fasces and Corporations, most of whose membership was elected or appointed from the corporations, took its place.

The duty of the corporations was to settle equably questions about working conditions within each vocation. Unfortunately, real equality between capital and labor did not prevail. Whereas the former was represented by traditional spokesmen, the latter was spoken for by middle-class lawyers and a handful of trade unionists compliant to the Fascist regime; the bulk of independent trade unionists had been forced out of public life. The only prominent Fascist genuinely sympathetic to worker rights and power, Edmondo Rossoni, was eased out as head of the Confederation of Fascist Trade Unions in 1928. Afterwards, the syndical labor representatives worked hand in glove with the industrialists who backed the Fascist regime, with the result that capital was kept on a very light rein while labor's freedom was heavily curbed. The corporative state in this way supplied the cloak for ruthless labor exploitation. In addition, the National Council of Corporations and Ministry of Corporations on paper helped to determine national economic policy. In practice, throughout the corporative structure Fascist party officials sat alongside the syndical representatives in order to lay down the party line. Corporative agencies merely approved decisions taken elsewhere, usually in the Fascist Grand Council.

But, if ineffectual, the corporative system provided an arsenal of bureaucratic jobs for the party faithful. Furthermore, many of these place-holders, in collusion with much of the business community, found in the corporative state opportunities for embezzlement on a grand scale. Most celebrated in this respect were the relatives and friends of Clara Petacci. Mussolini was always indulgent toward dishonesty in others—perhaps it satisfied his craving to feel superior—so the Petacci clan and similar parasites flourished unchecked.

This plunder of the national treasury under Fascism went beyond anything experienced in liberal Italy, although financial scandals in high places inevitably suggest some similarity between the two regimes. The parliamentary dictators of the pre-1914 era and the Fascist Duce alike were greedy for power, not wealth, and lived fairly austere lives. Yet, the machinery of both the liberal and the Fascist corporative state was oiled by bribes, the sale of favors, and corruption in general.

In sum, then, corporative theory constituted a not unintelligent reaction to the fragmentation of modern society. It was the instrument whereby the more enlightened elements within and close to Fascism hoped to effect national modernization. Bottai's *Critica Fascista,* the most cerebral of the regime's journals, provided a forum for debate over the proper implementation of corporativism, particularly the relationship among business, labor, the P.N.F., and the Duce's personal dictatorship. But in the last resort, it was the failure to reconcile these disparate parts of the national equation—coupled with Mussolini's growing preoccupation in the 1930s with imperial glory at the expense of domestic change—that rendered illusory the dream of a viable corporative state. David Roberts in *The Syndicalist Tradition and Fascist Italy* (1979) goes to the heart of the matter when he terms those petty bourgeois syndicalists who became the resident intelligentsia of Mussolini's corporative system the "myth makers" of the Fascist regime.

At least the lip service paid to corporativism indicated that Fascism would have no scruples about intervening in Italy's economic processes. In attracting support from Italian technocrats and "productivists," early Fascist rhetoric had clearly implied some degree of national economic planning. Indeed, after 1922, technical councils were set up to promote economic rationalization and efficiency. But they quickly faded into insignificance, starved as they were of encouragement from the upper levels of government where

Mussolini's first finance minister, Alberto De' Stefani, was an orthodox laissez-faire theorist. In 1925, however, he was replaced by Giuseppe Volpi, who ushered in a new economic era. Volpi was a spokesman for commerce and industry, and molded state action for the benefit of these interests. Higher tariffs, lower corporate taxes, and government contracts provided another likeness to liberal Italy, wherein the nexus between government and capital had been notoriously close. The trend to government patronage of selected businesses was quickened by the Great Depression of the early 1930s, the most notable innovation being the *Istituto per la ricostruzione industriale* (I.R.I.), a state-financed rescue operation for shaky concerns. For the most part, the big companies received I.R.I. help, while small businesses were allowed to go to the wall. Not surprisingly, economic centralization and cartelization grew apace. By 1939, it has been calculated, the I.R.I. umbrella covered 77 percent of Italy's pig-iron production, 80 percent of her naval construction, and 90 percent of the nation's shipping.

The Duce was fundamentally ignorant of economics. He personally fostered a number of schemes, but Italy's economic health usually had to play second fiddle to his perennial concern for prestige and propaganda. Thus, in 1926, Mussolini insisted that for reasons of national pride the international value of the lira be kept up. Its stabilization by the end of 1927 at an artificially high rate created endless difficulties for Italian exporters and serious deflation at home. Similarly, land reclamation was at the mercy of the Duce's showmanship. The Pontine Marshes, close to Rome and within the purview of foreign visitors, were the subject of a model project. But elsewhere money and good intentions were dissipated by dishonest contractors. And the *Mezzogiorno*, where land reclamation was crucial, remained sunk in poverty.

Mussolini liked to present his economic plans as mililtary campaigns. Hence, the "battle for births," although Italy was grossly overpopulated in relation to her economic resources and her main emigration outlet in the New World had just been closed. Then there was the "battle for grain," whereby increased domestic production enabled grain imports to be cut by 75 percent between 1925 and 1935. On the other hand, this was accomplished at the cost of reducing Italy's total agricultural output because so much land suitable for fruit or grazing was foolishly planted with wheat. Both these "battles" were launched in support of a militarist foreign policy. Mussolini openly admitted that the goal of his demographic campaign was more cannon fodder; the concentration on grain stemmed from the desire for self-sufficiency, or autarchy, in case of war. After the League of Nations briefly imposed economic sanctions on Italy in 1935–1936, the Fascist drive for autarchy accelerated. This determination to put the country on a war footing led inexorably to further government intervention in the national economy—through the I.R.I. and other "parastatal" agencies in which public and private capital joined to stimulate the discovery and exploitation of raw materials. Between 1934 and 1936, banking and foreign exchange were brought under the regime's tight central control. By the outbreak of the Second World War, there was not a little dismay in the Italian business community at the scope of this economic *dirigisme*.

Mussolini's economic policies were of such dubious inspiration that a consistent pattern of growth could hardly be expected. Indeed between 1925 and 1938, due to a combination of the Great Depression and Fascist ineptitude, Italy's national income rose a mere 15 percent; on a per capita basis the increase was only 10 percent. In the two years before Italy's entry into the Second World War, the national income rose faster, but this was due to the artificial stimulus of war preparations. Overall, the annual growth rate was far too small to support the budget deficits and the substantial increase in the public debt during the 1930s. The cost of the failure of Mussolini's economic policies was passed on to the lower classes, people of property and the middle class not feeling the pinch until the years of autarchy. Early on, labor was left vulnerable by the Fascist reversal of working-class gains made in the pre-Fascist era—gains such as the eight-hour factory day and checks on eviction and rack-renting in the countryside. On paper, both the

Fascist Charter of Labor in 1927 and the Charter of Mazzadria in 1933 (concerning rural share tenancy) struck a balance between property and labor. But the former's stipulation of worker rights was nonbinding on employers, while the latter's provisions too often went unheeded, especially in the unreconstructed South. Unemployment in Mussolini's Italy was always high and in the Great Depression stood at well over a million. In 1927, the government ordered across-the-board wage reductions, which were only partially restored when prices rose drastically in the later 1930s. The index of real wages fell between 1925 and 1938 by some 11 percent. The consumption of basic foodstuffs by the workers also dropped during the 1930s, succeeded by an inevitable decline in the level of public health. To a small extent, these miseries were offset by fringe benefits—governmental social services, recreational facilities, pensions, a reduced work week (although this last amounted to a wage cut for many). All this, however, was of marginal concern to Mussolini, who rationalized away the issue of living standards with the argument that material luxuries sapped the national vigor.

Fascism's shabby record in grappling with Italy's chronic economic difficulties stands in sharp contrast to its handling of another problem which had plagued Italy since unification—that of church-state relations. With liberal Italy's destruction of the last remnant of the papacy's temporal power in 1870, the pope had withdrawn as a "prisoner in the Vatican." He had refused to recognize the kingdom of Italy, rejected any settlement offered by the liberal government, and required all Italian Catholics to hold aloof from the secular state. Understandably, the rift between church and state inhibited thousands of devout Catholics from giving full allegiance to the unitary Italian state. Therefore, the reconciliation under Fascist auspices in 1929 known as the Lateran Accords denoted a signal contribution to national unity.

Although Mussolini could justly claim much credit for the Lateran Accords, he did not build them from scratch as he liked to pretend. By 1922, while the church-state relationship continued nominally one of mutual hostility, in practice a convenient *modus vivendi* had developed. The state had long since ceased to obstruct the Vatican's appointment of bishops. Nor did the courts enforce the legal restrictions on land-holding by the church. Church wealth was increasing, and clerical influence in Italian society showed no signs of dwindling. Catholics participated in secular affairs, as the growth of white trade unions and the Popular party amply demonstrated. The liberal oligarchy and the Vatican drew together in common fear of socialism. During Orlando's premiership in 1919 the first tentative feelers for an official church-state *rapprochement* were put out. At most, then, Fascism speeded up what had already been started, and what was perhaps inevitable anyway.

Nevertheless, the Fascist regime was peculiarly well suited to bring about a reconciliation. For Fascism appealed to the instincts of the powerful conservative wing of Italian Catholicism, the constituency from which the later Clerico-Fascists would be drawn. Its strength lay in landed wealth, and in control of the Catholic press trust and of the main organ of Catholic finance, the Bank of Rome. Conservative Catholics naturally admired Fascist antibolshevism. They also sympathized with Fascism because it was ultranationalist; in the Libyan War of 1911 and even the First World War (which the Vatican formally condemned), Italy's Nationalists had won backing in conservative Catholic circles. This conservative Catholic influence was plainly discernible in the Vatican's covert support of Fascism in the March on Rome and the Matteotti affair. It was still more evident in Pope Pius XI's supreme gesture of goodwill to Mussolini's regime—his acquiescence in the Fascist dissolution of Catholic trade unions and cooperatives and in the demise of the Popular party. Mussolini, as part of his campaign to woo the conservative Italian establishment, had begun to appease the Vatican with words as early as May 1920. Once in power, action followed: among other measures the crucifix and catechism were restored in elementary schools, Milan's Catholic university was officially recognized, and state allowances for priests were raised.

The feasibility of a church-state treaty seems to have been recognized from the moment Mussolini took office. In January 1923, the Duce and Cardinal Gasparri, the papal secretary of state, held a secret meeting. But not until the Fascist regime was firmly established in 1926 did formal negotiations open. They lasted three years, and on the Fascist side were closely supervised by Mussolini. The Lateran Accords of February 11, 1929, comprised three agreements. A convention dealt with a financial settlement for the church. A treaty guaranteed the sovereign independence of the Vatican City, and in return the Vatican accorded *de jure* recognition to the Italian state. Included in the treaty was a reconfirmation of the clause in the Italian constitution that recognized Catholicism as "the sole religion of the state." But the most important and extensive document was the concordat, which spelled out the church's new status in some detail, and through which most of the anticlerical legislation of the liberal era was repealed. The papacy obtained great freedom in episcopal appointments and substantive jurisdiction over marriages and wills. Ecclesiastical corporations gained tax relief, and religious orders recovered legal entity. In education, church schools were put on the same footing as state institutions, and compulsory religious instruction was extended into all secondary schools. "In short," writes R. A. Webster in *The Cross and the Fasces* (1960), "Italy became a confessional state unique among the great powers of contemporary Europe."

On the basis of concrete gains, most would concede that the papacy emerged from the Lateran Accords a clear winner. But there is a contrary argument, intimated by A. C. Jemolo in his *Church and State in Italy, 1850–1950* (1960), that in an intangible way the church may have lost. Fascism was fundamentally antichristian; its emphasis on this world and its worship of force were decidedly alien to Christian teaching; its leaders were always anticlerical at heart. By its association with such a movement, the Vatican ran the danger of losing its soul for the sake of material profit. The compromise with Italian Fascism naturally inhibited the church. At worst, it seems to have stood in the way of the church taking a firmer stance than it did against the much greater evil of the Nazi variety of fascism. At the very least, it detracted from the church's ability to be heard when it did preach against the unchristian aspects of fascism.

Truth to tell, the Vatican after 1929 was quite prepared to speak up against Mussolini's regime in matters of sufficient gravity. Predictably enough, trouble arose over youth education. The concordat of 1929 specifically recognized the right of the lay organization, Catholic Action, to operate in this sphere. But two years later, Mussolini deemed Catholic Action to be too politically oriented and a rival to Fascist youth groups, so he unleashed a furious propaganda attack and decreed the dissolution of Catholic Action's youth groups. The pope responded bitterly in an encyclical, *Non abbiamo bisogno*. The Clerico-Fascists intervened to fabricate a compromise in September 1931 in which Catholic Action forswore political activity but remained intact. Indeed, although forced to proceed inconspicuously, Catholic Action—and similar lay Catholic groups in the universities—were able to supply the political education of a whole generation of Christian Democratic politicians, who took office in Italy after the Second World War. Between 1931 and 1938, relations between Mussolini and the Vatican were more or less undisturbed. But when Mussolini, in seeming imitation of Hitler, introduced racist laws into Italy, Pope Pius XI was explicit in denunciation. His successor in 1939, Pius XII, was closer to the Clerico-Fascists and muted the criticism somewhat. But even as the Vatican's diplomatic policy grew enigmatic, its continued opposition to racism in principle was widely known.

The important thing, however, was that in neither the Catholic Action nor the racist controversy was there any serious move to renounce the Lateran Accords. What mattered to ordinary Catholics around the world was that under Fascism church and state had reached a lasting settlement, not that they sometimes quarreled over its execution. Among the mass of Italians, especially in the Catholic countryside, the conciliation with the church did a great deal to offset Fascism's dismal economic record. Mussolini probably won more instant popularity by the Lateran Accords than by anything else he ever accomplished.

With the Lateran Accords, Mussolini completed his accommodation with the main elements of Italy's traditional power structure. During the next decade, his attention turned to the Italian masses and to the task of integrating them for the first time into the state. This was prompted not just by a perceived need to complete Fascism's "second wave," but also by the realities of the 1930s. Social stability was put at risk by the economic distress of the Depression years and demanded that attention now be paid to Italy's masses. Consequently, in 1931, Mussolini announced his intention of "reaching out to the people." Two years later, enrollment in the P.N.F. was opened up, and increasingly thereafter party membership became the prerequisite for a professional career. But the concentration was not so much on political mobilization. Rather, Fascist attitudes and values were to be inculcated through mass organizations outside the party and civic institutions. By operating at the grass roots of society and in the workplace, the aim was to influence a citizen's life in its totality. Victoria De Grazia's *The Culture of Consent* (1981), which deals with this stratagem, focuses on the *Dopolavoro*, the national organization of leisure and foremost among these new socializing agencies. Springing out of the Fascist syndicates of the 1920s, the Dopolavoro by 1936 came to number some 20,000 branches with an overall membership of two and three-quarter million (80 percent of salaried employees belonged, 20 percent of urban manual workers, but only 7 percent of the peasantry). Other "organizations of consent" included many veterans' associations. At the other end of the age scale, youth cadres abounded: the *Balilla* for boys of eight to fourteen years of age, the *Avanguardisti* for those fourteen to eighteen years old, and the *Giovani Fascisti* for those between eighteen and twenty-one. There were equivalent though not so highly regarded groups for girls.

Like every dictator who imagines his regime to be permanent, Mussolini took great heed of the rising generation. Thus, it was a matter of P.N.F. pride that by 1939 over 60 percent of those eligible in the north were enrolled in Fascist youth groups. School curriculum, needless to say, was laid down by the state, and teachers carefully watched by local party officials. University professors had to swear a loyalty oath to the regime, and the student body encouraged to enlist in the Fascist student organization, *Gioventù Universitaria Fascista* (G.U.F.). Each year in the 1930s, the G.U.F. staged *Littoriali*, competitions involving written and artistic presentations and oral debates, which served as a useful laboratory to appraise one segment of public opinion in Fascist Italy. The *Littoriali*, in fact, provided an opportunity, even encouragement, for criticism of the regime. And interestingly, plaints were regularly voiced about the failure of *fascismo-movimento* to deliver the promised social revolution, and the mean-spirited Achille Starace, the current P.N.F. secretary, was openly ridiculed as a symbol of what *fascismo-regime* had become. For some the *Littoriali* provided a passage to anti-Fascism; for the majority, however, the exercise in criticism signified an abiding faith that Fascism would yet be revivified to live up to their idealist expectations. Thus, in the words of E. R. Tannenbaum, *The Fascist Experience* (1972), the *Littoriali* "mobilized for Fascism as well as against it." An instructive parallel may be drawn between Italy's "generation of the *Littoriali*" and the youth of eastern Europe who, since 1945, have grown increasingly captious of their Iron Curtain regimes. In neither case can criticism be equated with repudiation of the prevailing system, and though change might be demanded, its accomplishment must be seen within the context of Fascism and communism, respectively.

The populist "reach-out" of the thirties encouraged Mussolini to indulge his penchant for propaganda. He often said that journalism, not politics, was his true métier, by which he meant the editorial rather than the reportorial kind of journalism. On becoming premier, he had handed over the editorship of *Popolo d'Italia* to his brother, Arnaldo; but when the latter died in 1931, he gladly resumed direction of the paper. However, exposure by newspaper was limited in Italy, where much of the population was still functionally illiterate. Mussolini reached his largest audience through handbills and posters; the walls of Italy became the bearers of countless Fascist slogans. On both radio and film, something of Mussolini's magnetic oratory came across; state money was poured into the development of radio and cinema in order to broaden the channels of propaganda. To bring all the mass media within his purview Mussolini invented a ministry of propaganda which, in 1937, was euphemistically rechristened the Ministry of Popular Culture (or Minculpop for short).

The propaganda message that was hammered at all Italians was a simple one: total obedience to constituted authority. (Not for nothing was the official Fasaist magazine entitled *Gerarchia*, meaning hierarchy.) Supreme Fascist authority was vested in the Duce, which gave rise to the ludicrous slogan: "Mussolini is always right." Discipline and obedience were necessary because Italian life was conceived in terms of struggle. Partly this was struggle against environment, to which the celebrated economic "battles" bore witness, but mostly it was struggle against external enemies because "nothing has ever been won in history without bloodshed." The Fascist credo, then, could be reduced to the injunction, "Believe! Obey! Fight!" The supreme Fascist virtues were Spartan, and great stress was put on physical vigor. Even the Fascist hierarchs were compelled to perform elementary gymnastics in public; as these were mostly middle-aged men, the result was often low comedy rather than a high example.

It goes without saying that this martial muscularity went hand in hand with a denial of women's equality. Fascism, especially after the *rapprochement* with the Catholic church, exalted the old-fashioned, patriarchal family (a microcosm of the authoritarian state), and attacked the middle-class female professional who was held responsible for a declining birthrate. Not only were rewards given to parents of large families but, in 1938, a quota was imposed on female employment—a device also intended to relieve the pressure of male white-collar unemployment. In reality, the twentieth century would not be halted, and during the Fascist era the statistics of female employment in Italy continued to rise, especially in the customary fields of elementary schoolteaching and nursing. Undaunted, Fascist propaganda went on lauding the peasant earth mother whose sole national contribution was to produce sons for war.

In a similar fashion, cultural pursuits were at the mercy of Mussolini's political ambitions. A Fascist Institute of Culture was established to spell out an authentic *"stile fascista"* in art, but found it difficult to arrive at a consistent exegesis. Alternately, it might be said that in this area, as in so many others, Fascist eclecticism allowed the coexistence of many heterogeneous schools of thought—from academic classicism to several shades of modernism. But Mussolini put all such argumentation into perspective when he complained that foreign tourists were more impressed by Italy's art treasures than by the modern war machine which Fascism was supposedly building. The Duce was bored by museums, for his preoccupations were overwhelmingly philistine.

In brief, then, the state into which the Fascists proposed to integrate the mass of Italians was a bleak one. It demanded sacrifice and duty, and held out the distant hope of national conquest and honor as reward. Its unity was less that of a civil community than of an army.

To induce such militaristic conformity, the apparatus of a police state supplemented propaganda. In 1926, a Fascist secret police force was created under the acronym O.V.R.A.; what these letters stood for was left unclear (perhaps deliberately in order to create an aura of mystery and menace), but the most informed guess was *Opera Vigilanza Repressione Antifascista*. The same year saw the establishment of the Special Tribunal for the Defense of the State. Fascist justice operated for the most part secretly and arbitrarily, and was not averse to the use of torture. On the other hand, the death sentence was seldom imposed on political offenders. The standard punishment was *confino*. This could mean incarceration, often on one of the penal islands off Italy's coast. Here conditions were harsh, although in no way commensurate with those in Nazi concentration camps. Yet some did die in Fascist prisons. Probably, Fascist Italy's most famous political prisoner was the communist intellectual, Antonio Gramsci, whose prison writings have now become a text for all modern Marxists. Gramsci had been held in Fascist prisons for over ten years when he was finally released in 1937, desperately ill, to die a few days later. Alternatively, *confino* might involve banishment to a remote mainland district, where one could live a normal life, albeit under the surveillance of the local police. The vast disparity between one region of Italy and another made this a more severe penalty than it might seem at first thought. The psychological frustration of an enforced sojourn in a primitive, disease-ridden southern village has been hauntingly captured in the memoir, *Christ Stopped at Eboli* (1947) by Carlo Levi, an anti-Fascist artist from Turin sentenced to this type of *confino* in 1935.

The Fascist regime used terror, but was not in any real sense based on terror. Indeed, Fascist violence was more in evidence before 1925 than afterwards. This was not due to any increase of scrupulousness but to a decline in overt opposition. After 1925, the most vocal criticism of Fascism by Italians came from those mostly intellectual members of the upper and middle classes who were either driven into exile, or took refuge abroad of their own accord. These *fuorusciti* or outsiders—the word was used derisively by Mussolini, proudly by the expatriates themselves—included a galaxy of illustrious Italian names: the ex-premier Nitti; the former foreign minister, Count Sforza; almost the entire roster of past and future Socialist leadership—Turati, Treves, Nenni, Saragat; the first party secretary of the *Popolari,* Don Sturzo; the historian Salvemini; the physicist Enrico Fermi; Arturo Toscanini, who had run for parliament in 1919 as a Fascist candidate but rebelled in no uncertain fashion when he was required to play the Fascist song, *Giovinezza,* at his concerts. The *fuorusciti* may have damaged Fascism's reputation abroad, although how much is debatable. But their capacity to disturb the stability of Mussolini's regime at home was negligible.

Within Italy, anti-Fascist activity, while far from absent, was successfully contained by the regime. There was the occasional individual gesture. In 1931, the writer, Lauro De Bosis, showered Rome with anti-Fascist leaflets from the air, and immediately thereafter disappeared—probably because his plane crashed. Oddly enough, Mussolini tolerated one domestic dissenter. This was Benedetto Croce, who, after the Matteotti affair, broke with Fascism by sponsoring a Manifesto of Anti-Fascist Intellectuals (in reply to a pro-Fascist manifesto orchestrated by Giovanni Gentile.) The Duce considered Croce either too important to silence or, more likely, too ineffectual to be dangerous. Moreover, Croce's freedom of speech served as a rejoinder to foreign critics of the Fascist dictatorship. But Croce's was a voice in the wilderness. Out of 1,200 professors, only 11 refused to take the oath of loyalty, and they were forced into retirement and silence. Italian working-class movements were hamstrung by the imprisonment or exile of much of their traditional bourgeois leadership. On the other hand, the communists managed to keep a network of cells in being, and recent research in Fascist police files has disclosed a good deal of illegal strike activity, factory-floor slowdowns, riots by the unemployed, and rural tax revolts—most of which the regime was able to cover up at the time. This subterranean current of worker discontent, though, constituted no serious threat to Fascist rule—at least not until the years of war and defeat brought matters to a head. In the thirties, generally and outwardly the Italian masses remained quiescent, a condition very well conveyed in a work of fiction, Ignazio Silone's classic *Bread and Wine* (1937). The novel's hero is a *fuoruscito* who returns to Fascist Italy in 1935, the year of the Ethiopian war, and the plot turns on his failure to rouse either urban workers or peasants to insurrection. Silone was a member of the communist underground until 1930 when he was drummed out of the P.C.I. and took refuge in Switzerland. But he kept up his contacts with individual anti-Fascists inside Italy, and he knew whereof he wrote.

Without doubt, the time span encompassing the Lateran Accords and the Ethiopian war comprised Mussolini's halcyon years. The volume of De Felice's biography covering this period bears the subtitle *Gli anni del consenso, 1929–1936 (The Years of Consensus)*. Published in 1974, the book created a storm, not just in scholarly quarters, but in Italy's mass media. For De Felice called into question some of the shibboleths of the Italian Left bequeathed by the anti-Fascist resistance of 1943–1945. His contention that Mussolini may for a while have won the approbation of Italians at large challenged the imperative claim of the resistance that they, and never the Fascists, were the true representatives of the Italian people. This, coupled with De Felice's detection of a reformist strain in Fascism under the rubric of *fascismo-movimento,* incited Italy's Marxists, always since 1945 prominent in academe and journalism, to a fury. (Paradoxically, in the thirties the Italian communist line, epitomized in Palmiro Togliatti's *Lectures on Fascism* [Eng. trans. 1976] delivered in Moscow in 1935, had ruefully acknowledged Fascist dynamism and ability to marshal mass opinion.) The vituperation ceased only when Giorgio Amendola, one of the most respected of communist intellectuals in postwar Italy, wrote in partial defense of De Felice. But significantly, by the time the smoke had cleared, De Felice himself had retreated to the position of asserting that the Fascist consensus of 1929 to 1936 was a "passive" not an "active" one.

While Mussolini had grounds for self-congratulation on the public's acceptance of his regime, the Italian masses did not habitually show their ingrained cynicism toward the central authority in Rome on the surface. Through the ages they had learned to adapt to political change with the minimum of fuss. There is an Italian word *garbo,* untranslatable really but connoting recognition of the inevitable and adjustment to it with tact and discretion. Luigi Barzini in his national character sketch, *The Italians* (1964), places it in a political context: "It is, for instance, the careful circumspection with which one slowly changes political allegiance when things are on the verge of becoming dangerous." In this wise, the Italian masses became Fascist, with resignation not enthusiasm. There was little expectation that Mussolini's regime of gestures and promises would substantially change the way of life of the ordinary Italian. The popular practice of *garbo* deluded Mussolini into believing that he had bridged the gap between people and state. The true situation is epitomized in a story dating from the Fascist era. A high Fascist official visited a factory and asked the manager: "What are these workers' politics?" "One third communist, one third socialist, and the rest belong to small parties," was the reply. "What!" cried the livid Fascist: "Is none of them Fascist?" The manager hastened to reassure him: "All of them, Your Excellency, all of them."

At this point, it is necessary to pose a cardinal question about the Fascist dictatorship in Italy. Was it totalitarian?

There is no doubt that the Fascists aspired to totalitarianism. The Mussolini-Gentile article on Fascism in the *Enciclopedia italiana* reads:

> The Fascist conception of the state is all-embracing; outside of it no human or spiritual values can exist, much less have value. Thus under-stood, Fascism is totalitarian, and the Fascist state—a synthesis and a unit inclusive of all values—interprets, develops, and potentiates the whole life of a people.

Mussolini often used the word totalitarian, but it should be borne in mind that he normally did so in a limited sense. Thereby he meant no more than the supremacy of Fascist party organs in all walks of national life, especially economics. Up to a point, this goal was attained in Mussolini's one-party state. But to the social scientists who, in the aftermath of the Second World War, forged the theoretical construct of totalitarianism, mere ubiquitous party influence was not enough. They postulated other and more exacting criteria. By these standards it is generally conceded that the Italian Fascist state in several regards fell short of totalitarianism—certainly as it was conceived and practiced contemporaneously in Hitler's Germany and Stalin's Russia.

The *Enciclopedia italiana* itself, again under the heading of Fascism, offers a further test of totalitarianism: "No individuals or groups (political parties, cultural associations, economic unions, social classes) outside the state." But in fact, groups, classes, and institutions did maintain their identity in Fascist Italy. The most obvious were the church and the monarchy. The most authoritative work on Italian Fascist totalitarianism, Alberto Aquarone's *L'organizzazione dello Stato totalitario* (1965), states flatly: "The Fascist state proclaimed itself constantly and with great vocal exuberance a totalitarian state; but it remained until the end a dynastic and Catholic state, and therefore not totalitarian." In addition, behind the corporative facade the *Confindustria* and the *latifondisti* perpetuated their oligarchic entities. The armed forces, too, especially the navy, kept a good measure of autonomy under Mussolini. (The civilian bureaucracy, on the contrary, fell pretty heavily under Fascist control.) The phenomenon of independent subgroups was illustrated in microcosm in Sicily where the Fascists launched a drive against the local power structure, the *mafia*. During the Fascist era, the *mafia* was almost completely quiescent, and many *mafiosi* enlisted in the Fascist party. None the less, in July 1943 when the Allies landed in Sicily, the *mafia* reemerged into the open. In the western part of the island, it was influential enough to persuade most of the Italian troops to defy orders from Rome, and to lay down their arms to save the local villages from destruction.

Mussolini came to terms with these groups from the monarchy to the *mafia*. But at most he neutralized them; he neither annihilated nor absorbed them. They outlived his regime, and their existence undercut the Fascist claim to totalitarianism.

A totalitarian state cannot be content with outward conformity. If it were, it would be no more than a traditional Caesarian dictatorship. A totalitarian state requires the mental, not merely the physical, allegiance of its subjects. The dearth of popular enthusiasm behind Fascism's rise to power could be explained away; it was the function of an elite to appreciate the general will sooner than the multitude. But a totalitarian elite, once in power, had to convert the masses to its view of the general will. This was the purpose of all the indoctrination. Yet the Fascists failed to overcome the national trait of skepticism which had frustrated their liberal forerunners; Mussolini himself sorrowfully admitted that a whole generation would have to pass before the "new man" of Fascism could be manufactured in quantity. At the close of the Second World War, Germany endured the trauma of the Nuremberg Trials and denazification, while Italy underwent only a mild dose of *defascistizzazione*. Many factors contributed to this distinction, but among them certainly was a tacit recognition that social conditioning in Fascist Italy, compared to that in Nazi Germany, had been a shallow and deficient process.

The nature of the Fascist Italian consensus precluded totalitarianism in another respect. Dependence on a series of compromises with interest groups and *fiancheggiatori* (flankers), rather than on mass mobilization and grass-roots enthusiasm, bred what one writer has called "hyphenated fascism," a hybrid phenomenon necessarily devoid of a clear-cut ideology. A genuine totalitarian movement requires some quintessential set of ideas to guide and justify all its actions, and it is difficult to isolate any such driving faith at the core of Italian Fascism. Some have contended that the worship of action for its own sake and Mussolini's opportunism ruled out the possibility of a coherent ideology. Ernst Nolte, for one, in his translated work, *Three Faces of Fascism* (1965) emphasizes "the priority of action over doctrine" in Fascist Italy. Nolte is probably too harsh, if only because he ignores corporativism. Corporativism might have been a viable Italian Fascist ideology, but of course, Mussolini himself did not live up to it. Other writers have seen an ideology in the "idea of Rome." The notion of Mussolini's Italy as heir to the Rome of the Caesars and the Popes loomed larger in Fascist propaganda in proportion as corporativism and the veiled promise of social and economic change receded; it marked the regime's shift in priorities from domestic policy in the twenties to international affairs in the thirties. The dream of a Third Rome and past glories reborn had the simple and mythical quality that Sorel, whom Mussolini hailed as his mentor, held necessary to excite large numbers to action. The trouble with "the idea of Rome" as a totalitarian ideology, however, was that it lacked any cosmic relevance—unlike the sentiments of race and class which informed the Nazi and communist movements. Rather, it sounded suspiciously like a euphemism for old-fashioned Italian patriotism; indeed, liberal Italy before 1914 had initially given tongue to the conceit of a Third Rome. Here, it may be appropriate to quote Hannah Arendt's verdict on Fascist Italy in her seminal work, *Origins of Totalitarianism* (1951): "Not totalitarian, but just an ordinary nationalist dictatorship."

Indeed, since 1915, by far the most consistent thread running through Mussolini's career had been his attachment to the nationalist cause. One wonders, therefore, whether, for the Duce, totalitarianism was not so much an end in itself as an instrument in the service of Italian nationalism. Totalitarian unity at home was required because it was anticipated that the pursuit of a nationalist foreign policy would sooner or later involve Italy in war. Ironically, when that happened in 1940, the Second World War brutally exposed the shortcomings of Italian Fascist totalitarianism.

5
Fascist Diplomacy

It has been observed in an earlier chapter that many Italians welcomed Fascism because it seemed to offer solutions to two specific problems—namely, the red menace and the "mutilated victory." Both were to a great extent mythical. The latter, however, was a symptom of a larger, more substantive difficulty. The injustice meted out to Italy in the postwar settlement was undeniably exaggerated by Italian opinion. Nevertheless, there did exist in international circles a definite tendency to disparage Italy summed up in such catch-phrases as "the least of the great powers" or "the sixth wheel of European diplomacy." Italy simply did not possess the wherewithal to be a major power of the first rank. For instance, Italy's surplus population was of little military value, due to nutritional and educational deficiencies. Italy could not feed herself and was particularly dependent on supplies of foreign grain. Still more important, nearly all Italy's coal and raw iron came from abroad. Thus Italy was put in the grip of whichever power controlled the entrances to the Mediterranean through which lay the natural routes of imports. Similarly, Italy's long coastline left her open to invasion by a superior naval force. Of course, Great Britain, with her stranglehold on Gibraltar and Suez and her formidable Mediterranean fleet based on Malta, was the power that Italy had to take most into account. The coordination of British and French naval strength before 1914 had given Italy further pause for thought. Her intervention in the First World War on the Anglo-French side had been not unrelated to the Mediterranean balance of power. The

77

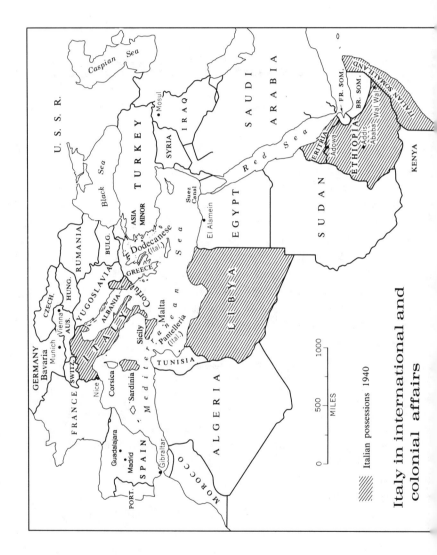

Italian possessions 1940

Italy in international and
colonial affairs

Foreign Ministry's traditional view of Italy's international position is to be found expressed, fancifully but frankly, in the *Ricordi* (1950) of one of its prominent officials, Raffaele Guariglia:

> . . . historically constrained, for intrinsic and obvious reasons, to take her stand first on one side and then on the other; to pursue the execution of her aims by cutting from the garments of her adversaries the material necessary for her own cloak; and to take refuge on rainy days (so long as this cloak was not ready) under the ample and capacious mantle of England.

It was this perpetual deference to stronger powers that Mussolini was pledged to stop. Before 1922, the taunt of *rinunciatari* (renouncers) had helped to speed the liberals out of power. If Mussolini did not play the nationalist hero, he might be supplanted by another. Hence, Mussolini kept a wary eye on his potential rival, D'Annunzio. (He placated the elderly patriot with honors and even provided him with an official gatekeeper to turn away unwelcome tourists. This worthy was, in fact, a police spy who reported sedulously to the Duce.) Mussolini plunged energetically into the task of sublimating hypernationalist sentiment. Immediately on coming to power, he stated Fascist Italy's claim to parity with the other European powers in the formula *"niente per niente"* (nothing for nothing.) It was to break out of Italy's traditional diplomatic limits that the Fascist experiment in an autarchic and martial society was launched. In the last resort, therefore, Italy's international status was to be the measure by which Mussolini's regime would stand or fall.

Many, both in Italy and abroad, who had qualms about Fascist diplomacy, put their trust in the capacity of the Italian Foreign Ministry to curb Mussolini. The career diplomats were nationalistic enough to want to use the threat of Fascist aggressiveness to frighten Britain and France into concessions. On the other hand, they aimed, in Guariglia's words, "to present to the world the Man [Mussolini] as capable of bringing new strength to our country, but without transgressing the bounds of international life." Yet apart from Mussolini's first year or so in office, the opinion of the old guard at the Foreign Ministry counted for very little. There was not really a clash of wills; Italy's diplomats were supportive enough of a forceful foreign policy, but the Duce all too often ignored his professional advisers. He used secret agents for his diplomatic intrigues, and sometimes Italy's diplomats were not even aware of what Fascist foreign policy was. An inert pessimism settled on the Italian diplomatic corps. In 1926, Salvatore Contarini, who as secretary-general of the Foreign Ministry was the dean of the permanent officials, tendered his resignation, most likely because his self-esteem was affronted by Mussolini's neglect. Contarini's departure came shortly after the elevation of Dino Grandi, the former *ras* of Bologna, to the office of undersecretary of foreign affairs. He appeared to be Mussolini's man chosen to impose Fascist conformity on the Foreign Ministry. But Grandi confounded this expectation by adopting the manners and views of the career diplomats. Astonishingly, the Duce tolerated this, even making Grandi foreign minister in 1929. But three years later, Grandi fell from favor; his espousal of general disarmament through the League of Nations was deemed un-Fascist, and he was packed off to the London embassy, for he had also evolved into an ardent Anglophile. Mussolini himself took back the foreign affairs portfolio.

In the 1930s, the Foreign Ministry, like the rest of the bureaucracy, grew more Fascist. A few diplomats retained their independence and told Mussolini what he did not like to hear. Ambassador Attolico in Nazi Berlin was outstanding in this respect. But generally such men were heeded no more than Contarini and Grandi earlier. The apotheosis of diplomacy under Mussolini was reached in 1936 with the appointment of Count Galeazzo Ciano as foreign minister. Aged thirty-three, Ciano was the son of one of the first Fascists and the husband of Mussolini's daughter, Edda. He possessed a certain perceptiveness in political matters. But in personality he was a lightweight and a thorough product of the Fascist system. He seldom contradicted the Duce even when he judged his policies ruinous. Mussolini was, thus, unhindered in making Fascist foreign policy. Whether he held the post formally or not, he was in reality his own foreign minister during the entire Fascist era.

It used to be said that the years 1922 to 1932 were "a decade of good behavior" by Fascist Italy in international affairs. But this was a superficial estimate. It is true that the consolidation of Fascist power at home distracted from diplomatic adventures and innovation. However, these were far from absent.

In September 1923, Fascist Italy seized the Greek island of Corfu, strategically located where the Adriatic flows into the Mediterranean. This involved Mussolini in a brush with the League of Nations, to which the Greeks immediately appealed. Mussolini rather relished the confrontation between Italian nationalism and the spokesmen for internationalism at Geneva whom he despised. He made plans to withdraw Italy from the League. An outright clash was prevented, however, by the French, who feared the League's cognizance of the Corfu crisis might be a precedent to interference in the French occupation of the German Ruhr. The French shifted the Corfu question to the Conference of Ambassadors, a preserve of the major Allied powers. This body came up with a *realpolitik* solution. Avowedly, Italy had taken Corfu as a pledge of reparation for the assassination on Greek soil of some Italian officials attached to an international commission delimiting the Albanian boundary. The Conference of Ambassadors fixed reparation at the considerable sum of fifty million lire. In reality, Mussolini's intention was to annex Corfu, and he had no wish to sell the island back to Greece at any price. It required a thinly veiled British threat to use the Mediterranean fleet before Fascist Italy evacuated Corfu. The Corfu affair was dispatched in less than a month and was quickly forgotten. But it constituted a dress rehearsal for the more momentous crisis over Ethiopia a dozen years later. In both cases, Fascist expansion ran afoul of the League, whose action was undercut by the British and the French.

Mussolini fared better in Fiume than at Corfu. Two weeks after the Corfu occupation, he sent a military commandant to govern Fiume. The explanation from Rome was that negotiations to found an independent Fiume were at an impasse, and that the town was falling into anarchy. Yugoslavia accepted the coup because France, Yugoslavia's protector, was too absorbed with the Ruhr occupation to do anything; and also because King Alexander of Yugoslavia, by nature an authoritarian, admired Mussolini for his domestic policy. In January 1924, Mussolini won a great *succès d'estime*. A settlement with Yugoslavia gave the bulk of Fiume to Italy; this was accompanied by an Italo-Yugoslav friendship pact. At one and the same time, Mussolini outdistanced both D'Annunzio and the *rinunciatari*. Actually, in the long run this turned out to be a Pyrrhic victory. Within two years, Rome and Belgrade were at odds again— this time over each other's ambition in Albania. Moreover, the Yugoslavs developed Split as an outlet for their commerce, and by 1940, grass was growing in the streets of Italian Fiume.

Fascist Italy's failure to hold Corfu and her success in acquiring Fiume had been due, in the final analysis, not to Greece and Yugoslavia, but to the reactions of Britain and France. This touched on the crucial question for Fascist foreign policy. How far could Mussolini follow a nationalist and expansionist course and at the same time remain within the framework of the First World War alliance with Britain and France? If Mussolini was to relieve his country's national inferiority complex at all, he was bound to offer some defiance to London and Paris, whose governments were held primarily responsible for the "mutilated victory." This carried with it a further implication. International politics between the wars evinced a distinct polarization. On the one side were the victors of the First World War, anxious to preserve the status quo which they had established in 1919. On the other, there were the defeated powers whose attitude to the peace treaties was understandably revisionist. The further Mussolini moved away from Britain and France, the closer he was likely to gravitate to the opposing camp of revisionist states. So by the nature of the diplomatic problem, Fascist Italy was beset from the beginning by the temptation of international revisionism.

Mussolini's attitude to Great Britain was ambivalent. He came to enjoy genial personal relations with a variety of British statesmen, ranging from the Conservative Winston Churchill to the Labor party leader, Ramsay MacDonald. He was most friendly, however, with Sir Austen Chamberlain, the Conservative foreign secretary between 1924 and 1929. (It is ironic that Austen, who humored Mussolini in the twenties, was the stepbrother of Neville Chamberlain, who tried to appease Hitler in the next decade.) This personal cordiality was translated into a modest political entente. Fascist Italy helped to put pressure on Turkey, which won the oil town of Mosul for the British mandate of Iraq. In return, Britain cleared the way for a virtual Italian protectorate over Albania. Both had a vested interest in combating Pan-Islamism, which threatened their colonial empires. On the other hand, Britain and Italy were colonial rivals, and Mussolini was painfully aware of this. He never forgot that those British conservatives who admired his antibolshevism could also be the implacable foes of Italian imperialism. "It is a great illusion to think that the English Conservative government is a sincere friend of Italy," he warned his cabinet in 1929. Mussolini's feelings about Britain and her empire recalled those of William II of Germany before 1914—grudging admiration mingled with malicious envy. And like the Kaiser, Mussolini found his envy hard to control, resulting in a strong streak of Anglophobia.

Mussolini was jealous of France too, although in this case his enmity showed plainly and consistently from the start. He took a Social Darwinian view of relations between the so-called Latin sisters. Competition between them was inevitable, even healthy. One power was always on the rise and certain to dominate the other in decline. Now Fascism had supposedly invigorated the Italian national organism, while the French people, in Mussolini's opinion, were "truly decadent." According to this scheme of things, Italian influence was destined ultimately to replace that of France in the western basin of the Mediterranean.

Excuses to pick a quarrel were not lacking. In the French protectorate of Tunisia, there were more Italians than French *colons*. The French authorities perennially threatened to abrogate the rights of these Italians, a procedure which kept all Italian nationalists in a state of high indignation. Mussolini himself made more of another issue—that of the *fuorusciti,* who congregated heavily in Paris. To each Italian complaint at their anti-Fascist propaganda, the French government responded with a reference to the constitutional right of free speech in a democracy. Mussolini retaliated by sending his own agents into France to operate clandestinely against the *fuorusciti.* In 1926, for instance, it was revealed that two grandsons of the famous Garibaldi, in Fascist pay, had been acting as *agents provocateurs* on French soil to involve the *fuorusciti* in a proposed invasion of Italy. An even more sensational episode concerned another pair of brothers, the Rossellis, active *fuorusciti* editors who, in 1937, were murdered near Paris by Fascist Italian agents. All in all, it is difficult to avoid the impression that Mussolini deliberately used the *fuorusciti* issue to foment ill will between Italy and France.

Mussolini's Francophobia led him to approach France's principal enemy and the major revisionist power, namely, Germany. At the time of his Fiume coup, when he feared that France might come to Yugoslavia's aid, Mussolini suggested that Germany "immobilize part of the French army on the Rhine." Gustav Stresemann, the current German chancellor and foreign minister, turned down the one-sided overture. Whereupon, Mussolini conceived an extreme contempt for Stresemann and for the Weimar regime which he considered, quite incorrectly, to be run by socialists and pacifists. More perceptively, he forecast the advent to power one day of a German ultranationalist government. As insurance against this contingency, Mussolini sought to ingratiate himself with the German nationalists. Most notably, he sent military supplies to assist in Germany's secret rearmament. Of course, this was playing with fire. The German nationalists aspired to an *Anschluss* (union of Austria with Germany.) Once this was accomplished, the next step in the German revisionist program was to cross the Brenner and take over the Alto Adige—or as the Germans themselves preferred to call it, the South Tyrol. This was the region containing 200,000 Germans which Italy had acquired in 1919. Mussolini was alert to the Pan-German danger, and in 1925 he tried to have the Brenner included among those frontiers guaranteed in the Locarno Pacts. Unsuccessful in this, he compensated by never missing an opportunity to assert in public Italy's legal title to the Alto Adige.

Significantly, one German nationalist group was prepared to renounce the Alto Adige as the price for Fascist Italy's friendship. This was Hitler's Nazi party. Mussolini was at first unimpressed with the Nazis, calling them "buffoons." Nevertheless, he did not dismiss them entirely. He probably gave secret support to Hitler as the latter prepared for his first bid for power in November 1923. Certainly, after the abortive Munich beer hall *Putsch*, several Nazis found comfortable asylum in Fascist Italy.

Mussolini's gamble, then, was that by appeasing German nationalism, he could deflect it from the Alps to the Rhine. He thereby committed himself to the cause of revisionism, at least selectively. By 1928, he reached the point of endorsing the principle of revisionism in the open. "In the peace treaties," he told the Senate, "there are territorial, colonial, financial, and social clauses which should be discussed, reviewed, and improved in order to prolong the life of the treaties themselves and thus to assure a longer period of peace."

These words and Mussolini's entire strategy for coping with German revisionism were put to the test by Hitler's arrival in power in January 1933. This galvanized Mussolini into action. In March, he suggested that Italy, Britain, France, and Germany join together in a four-power pact. By this, Mussolini hoped to continue his policy of appeasing and containing Germany at the same time. His proposal offered Hitler parity of arms and hinted at revision of the territorial clauses of the 1919 settlement. On the other hand, it postulated a revival of the nineteenth-century concert of major European powers which, although including Germany, was to serve as a security measure against excessive Pan-German ambitions. This, of course, would have undercut the League of Nations system of collective security, a consideration not absent from Mussolini's calculations. However, it was the reference to revisionism which proved the stumbling block. Revisionism was contemplated plainly at the expense of Czechoslovakia and Poland, two key members of the French alliance system. The combined influence of Paris, Prague, and Warsaw was enough to emasculate Mussolini's plan. The Four-Power Pact, signed in Rome in June, made no mention of arms equalization or revisionism. In due course, the treaty was ratified only by Italy and Germany.

The danger to Italy of unrestrained German nationalism was amply demonstrated a year later. In July 1934, the Austrian Nazis assassinated Chancellor Dollfuss and tried to seize power in Vienna. Their avowed goal was union with Hitler's *Reich*. Although gravely apprehensive of an *Anschluss*, Fascist Italy was not without responsibility for the threat to Austria's independence. For many years, Mussolini had tried to keep Austria out of Germany's clutches by financing Austrian quasi-Fascists who were well-disposed toward Italy; Dollfuss himself was one such favorite. But Italian money and arms were used primarily to destroy the Austrian Social Democrats, who were the staunchest defenders of Austria's integrity against the Nazi menace. This inadvertent help from Rome notwithstanding, Austria's Nazis still needed the direct support of Berlin to come to power. Yet, if Hitler moved, it meant a clash with Fascist Italy. In 1934, Mussolini objected strenuously to *Anschluss*, and even mobilized some troops on the Brenner as though he might oppose it by force. Hitler in *Mein Kampf* and elsewhere had laid it down that Italian friendship was to be cultivated at any cost. (In his grand strategy, Italy was to neutralize the Anglo-French in the Mediterranean, while Germany gained land in central and eastern Europe.) Therefore, Hitler temporized in 1934. The Viennese Nazis were left to their own devices and their *Putsch* collapsed. Nonetheless, the threat of *Anschluss* was not removed. The mere presence of a nationalist regime in Berlin guaranteed that it would grow, not diminish, with time.

At this juncture, Mussolini chose to become embroiled in Africa. Since 1932, when he resumed direction of the Foreign Ministry and simultaneously banished Grandi and a handful of senior foreign service officials from Rome, Mussolini had been edging toward some kind of initiative on the world stage. The Third Rome mentality, fed increasingly by the Fascist regime's propaganda, looked primarily for satiation outside Europe. "Italy's historical objectives," declaimed the Duce in March 1934, "have two names: Asia and Africa. South and East are the cardinal directions which must excite the interest and will of Italians." Italian Fascism's grandiose design comprehended nothing less than an empire encompassing Asia Minor and North Africa from ocean to ocean, all made possible of course by Italian control of the Mediterranean (*mare nostrum*). Not for nothing did the walls of Fascist Rome carry maps of classical Rome's empire at its zenith. The acquisition of Ethiopia was to be but a first step in the realization of this scenario. It was always in the cards that Mussolini's nationalist regime would sometime try to avenge the defeat at Adowa in 1896, which had thwarted Italy's first bid to take over Ethiopia. In point of fact, Fascist military planning for war with Ethiopia got underway in 1932. An incident at Wal Wal on the border between Italian Somaliland and Ethiopia precipitated hostilities in December 1934, although Italy did not formally declare war on Ethiopia until the following October. It has, however, always been one of the puzzles of Fascist diplomacy why Mussolini thought the moment propitious, for his reaction to the danger across the Brenner in 1934 indicated that he was not blind to the peril of Italy's distraction from Europe.

To some extent, the answer must lie in Italy's domestic condition and Fascism's failure to cope with the Great Depression. Writes George Baer in *The Coming of the Italo-Ethiopian War* (1967): "The Ethiopian adventure was almost certainly contrived, at least in part, as an alternative to social reform." Or, in the same context, the Duce may have felt a need to provide an outlet for his military desperadoes; Salvemini in his contemporary *Under the Axe of Fascism* (1936) made a suggestive comparison between Mussolini's Ethiopian war and Hitler's bloodletting in the Night of the Long Knives on June 30, 1934. Yet, whatever pressures at home

Mussolini was subject to, there can be no question that the Italo-Ethiopian war arose principally from his appraisal of the international scene. Mussolini was driven constantly by his obsession with prestige, abroad as well as at home. Since 1933, the Duce was no longer senior Fascist, so to speak, and Hitler's mere accession to power had caused tremors in the diplomatic structure which Mussolini had never been able to induce. The Ethiopian venture, then, was in the nature of keeping up with a Fascist neighbor. In more concrete terms, E. M. Robertson's *Mussolini as Empire-Builder* (1977) reconstructs the European balance of power in 1934–1935 as it appeared in Rome, where the German problem was rationalized away by the calculation that a lightning victory could be won in Africa before German rearmament went into high gear and the *Anschluss* danger appeared imminent again. A quick and glorious victory, which by its very example might deter Hitler in Austria, was the essence of Fascist strategy. Moreover, Mussolini had reason to believe that he could count on the diplomatic support of Britain and France to facilitate his speedy conquest of Ethiopia. The British and French each possessed colonial territory contiguous with Ethiopia, and their attitude was necessarily of paramount concern to Mussolini.

In January 1935, the French foreign minister, Pierre Laval, visited Rome. Laval's aim was to create a united anti-German front in Europe; Mussolini was naturally preoccupied with African matters. At least an oral bargain was struck. Mussolini was agreeable to taking a firm anti-German stand, especially in Austria. In Africa, an accommodation was reached on the status of Italians in Tunisia. More important, Laval gave Italy some sort of green light in Ethiopia. Later, he was to protest that he approved only economic penetration. But this is hard to believe. Fascist Italy's designs on Ethiopia were clearly territorial, and Laval could hardly have failed to discern this when he encouraged Mussolini.

Over the years, Britain had actually shown more sympathy than France toward Italy's Ethiopian ambitions, although whether it would extend to approval of outright annexation had to be doubted.

At any rate, Mussolini needed an up-to-date token of London's good will before attacking Ethiopia in 1935. The occasion to obtain this arrived in the spring with Hitler's announcement of open German rearmament. In April, Britain, France, and Italy met at Stresa, a north Italian lake resort, to consider this development; the reunion of the First World War Allies on Italian soil testified to the functioning of the Laval-Mussolini agreement. The Stresa Conference, however, produced nothing but mild verbal reproof at Hitler's violation of the postwar settlement. On the other hand, it had a drastic impact on the tense Italo-Ethiopian crisis. The British delegation included two experts on Africa, who presumably expected to discuss Ethiopia with their Italian counterparts. But Mussolini refused to allow the subject to be raised, officially at any rate; and when the British did not insist, he promptly interpreted British silence as tacit endorsement of his Ethiopian schemes. In like vein, he construed the official Stresa communiqué, which contained the innocuous words "in Europe" after the standard pledge to uphold peace and the status quo, to imply approval of his African aggression. In all this, Mussolini was being deliberately devious as well as self-indulgent in wishful thinking. But a more substantive hint of British complaisance reached Rome during the summer. In June, a British interdepartmental committee under the chairmanship of Sir John Maffey reported that there existed "no vital British interests in Abyssinia or adjoining countries such as to necessitate British resistance to an Italian conquest of Abyssinia." A copy of this secret Maffey Report fell into the hands of Italian intelligence, and thus stiffened Mussolini's resolve.

By midsummer 1935, the Duce could not imagine that Britain and France would break the common front against Germany in order, as Sir Ivone Kirkpatrick, the British diplomat and biographer of Mussolini, puts it, "to prevent Italy from doing in Abyssinia what they themselves had done in Egypt and Morocco." This calculation was sound as far as it went. But, dictator that he was, Mussolini ignored the role of public opinion in a parliamentary democracy. This proved to be a particularly egregious error in the case of

Britain, for it was British opinion which in the main forced the League of Nations into the picture. Ethiopia had appealed to the League as early as January 1935, but the League feared to act without a lead from Britain and France. Coincidentally, at the end of 1934, the League of Nations Union had begun to canvass the British public's opinion of the League. Over eleven million participated in the so-called Peace Ballot. By June 1935, some ten million had expressed themselves in favor of the League as an instrument of collective security, although significantly only six million supported the use of military sanctions. This popular endorsement of the League, albeit qualified, weighed heavily on the British government, which was looking ahead to the next general election. It dared not openly give Mussolini carte blanche in Ethiopia lest it seem to betray the League. London made several overtures to find a compromise solution without involving the League. The most famous was the visit of Anthony Eden to Rome in June 1935. Eden offered Italy a slice of Ethiopian territory, for which London would compensate Ethiopia out of British Somaliland. The Duce rejected the plan outright.

By the time of the annual session of the League Assembly in September, the British government had to choose between appeasing Mussolini and satisfying the British people's attachment to the League. On the 11th, the British foreign secretary, Sir Samuel Hoare, addressed the Assembly. In the course of a carefully phrased speech, he said: "In conformity with its precise and explicit obligations the League stands, and my country stands with it, for the collective maintenance of the Covenant in its entirety, and particularly for steady and collective resistance to all acts of unprovoked aggression." Almost his entire audience interpreted this as blanket British support for League action against Fascist Italy, and jubilation reigned at Geneva. Hoare, who had not really intended to encourage the League, was taken aback. The next day, he assured Laval—who relayed the information to Mussolini—that in no circumstances would Britain contemplate military sanctions. (British policy was sticking close to the results of the Peace Ballot.) But

Hoare could not stop what he had started. When, on October 3, Fascist Italy invaded Ethiopia, the League was in a mood for sanctions. Britain and France were committed in principle, and both voted for the application of economic sanctions.

In reality, however, only limited sanctions were adopted; oil was left off the list of goods to be denied Italy and the Suez Canal was not closed. But even the modest sanctions applied were given no opportunity to succeed, for the whole League effort was quickly scuttled by the British and French. The British general election in November returned the government to office and freed it from the immediate need to defer to popular sympathy for the League. On December 7, Hoare met Laval in Paris and agreed to try to keep Mussolini within the anti-German front with the offer of two-thirds of Ethiopia. Within hours, the substance of the Hoare-Laval Pact appeared in the press, perhaps leaked by Laval himself. British public opinion was incensed at the desertion of the League, and the British government shortly saw fit to save face by disclaiming both Hoare and his pact.

Whether Mussolini would have negotiated on the basis of the Hoare-Laval plan is impossible to say. The revelation of the pact, though, removed any chance of concerted action against Italy. Thus, a major offensive in Ethiopia was launched with impunity in the new year 1936. The Italian tactics included the bombing of civilians and the use of poison gas—which aroused the conscience of a world still innocent enough to feel shock at such things. Among Italians, however, the war was immensely popular, not least because the church blessed the Fascist campaign as a "civilizing mission." (The Ethiopians were, in fact, Christian although not Roman Catholic.) Mussolini aroused patriotic fervor with his announcement of an intensified drive for autarchy to combat sanctions. Thousands of Italian women donated their wedding rings to the war effort. On May 5, the Ethiopian capital, Addis Ababa, was captured, and a few days later the King of Italy assumed the title, Emperor of Ethiopia. In July, the League put the seal on Fascist Italy's success by lifting sanctions.

But no sooner did Mussolini emerge from one war than he plunged into another. In July 1936, Spain's recently elected Popular Front government came under attack from Spanish right-wing elements, including the *Falange* (Spain's Fascist party). Italian help was sent immediately to the rebel leader, General Franco. Mussolini's motives were mixed: partly, he viewed intervention as an ideological crusade to save Spain from the alleged communism of the Popular Front; partly, he hoped a Franco government in Madrid might be an Italian puppet, thereby enabling Italy to challenge Anglo-French predominance in the western Mediterranean; and partly he imagined the Spanish battlefield would be a showcase for Fascist valor. On this last count, he was gravely disappointed, notably at Guadalajara where a numerically superior Italian force was defeated by a contingent of international volunteers, many of whom were anti-Fascist exiles. Mussolini's answer was to pump more resources into Spain; by 1937, Fascist Italy had 25,000 men in Spain. In the long run, however, Mussolini's greatest service to Franco lay in the provision of vast quantities of war matériel, nearly all of it on credit.

Italy's involvement in the Spanish Civil War far exceeded that of the other interventionists, Nazi Germany and Soviet Russia. Automatically, Mussolini was the major violator of the international nonintervention agreement to which he had subscribed in September 1936. Although criticism of Fascist Italy was rife in the democracies, Britain and France turned an official blind eye to Mussolini's misconduct. Only once in the summer of 1937, when Italian submarines began to prey on ships in Spanish waters, did London and Paris threaten to curb Italy. Mussolini at once put a stop to the acts of piracy. Despite the overwhelming weight of foreign intervention on the rightist side, the Spanish Civil War dragged on. Mussolini had anticipated a repetition of his swift Ethiopian triumph. But having committed his prestige to a Franco victory, he refused to draw back. Franco's control over all of Spain was not established until the spring of 1939. By then, Fascist Italy had paid a crushing price for intervention.

The Spanish Civil War injected a note of ideology into international affairs. At the time, many interpreted it as a confrontation between fascism and communism; others regarded it as the opening skirmish in a universal conflict between fascism and democracy. Mussolini was often swayed by such large-scale considerations. He really believed his own statements that this was "a century of Fascism." Where possible—in the United States for example—he tried to disseminate Fascist ideas through Italian immigrant communities. The international atmosphere created by the Spanish episode encouraged Mussolini's penchant for rigid, ideological thinking; in 1937, he readily aligned Fascist Italy with Germany and Japan in an anti-Comintern pact. Another sort of simplistic world-vision played its role in Mussolini's irrevocable breach with democratic Britain and France. In both the Ethiopian and Spanish crises he took close note of the half-hearted and vacillating Anglo-French policies. They appeared to confirm his prior diagnosis, compounded from anecdotal scandal to which he was addicted, of the effeteness of British and French ruling circles. In more cosmic terms, Mussolini now drew a sharp distinction between the "demoplutocracies"—allegedly "dying," "sterile" powers—and the "young," "prolific" nations on the march in Rome and Berlin. After 1936, such Social Darwinian fancies infused not just Fascist oratory but Fascist diplomacy too.

The discord with Britain was of particular consequence. From 1922 to 1935, Fascist Italy had been kept nominally loyal to the victorious alliance of the First World War by a loose Anglo-Italian entente. Its rupture could not help but push Mussolini further toward the international revisionists. In *realpolitik* terms, there was no reason why the entente should not have survived Ethiopia and Spain. In the last resort, Britain had not physically impeded Fascist Italy in either place. Nevertheless, Mussolini took umbrage at Britain, and particularly at what he considered British duplicity in dragging the League into the Ethiopian affair. "Fifty nations, led by one," he stormed. The blame for the failure to heal the rift rested more heavily on Italy than on Britain. London made overtures, sometimes fumbling, for a *rapprochement*. Mussolini went so far as to allow the oddly named Gentlemen's Agreements, confirming the status quo in the Mediterranean and the Red Sea, to be negotiated in 1937 and 1938. But the Italian signature meant nothing. And in the spring of 1939, Mussolini was studiously unmoved by Britain's supreme gestures to appease him—recognition of both Italy's Ethiopian empire and Franco's government in Spain. Such frigidity was, after all, no more than an admission of geopolitical realities; so long as Mussolini harbored vast imperial dreams, the British, standing sentinel over the Mediterranean at Gibraltar and Suez, constituted Fascist Italy's jailer and natural antagonist.

The reverse image of frayed Anglo-Italian relations was the thriving Rome-Berlin Axis. This was born in the fall of 1936. In October, Ciano and the German ambassador in Rome signed a secret protocol, pledging general cooperation in a variety of questions around the globe. Then Ciano traveled to Germany where he had an interview with Hitler laced with expressions of reciprocal good will. On November 1, Mussolini made the first public reference to "this Rome-Berlin line which is not a diaphragm but an axis around which can revolve all those European states with a will to collaboration and peace." The Axis was almost entirely an Italian invention. Naturally, Hitler was overjoyed, but he had done little consciously to bring it about. Indeed, in 1935–1936, Berlin was rather cool to Mussolini, feeling that his Ethiopian adventure weakened Italy's ability to play her allotted role alongside Nazi Germany in Europe. Mussolini contrived the Rome-Berlin Axis of his own free will, presumably calculating that it could be jettisoned if the need arose. In truth, the Axis at first was in no sense a firm political arrangement; like the Anglo-Italian entente which it superseded, it reflected simply a state of mutual tolerance and empathy. One school of thought, represented best perhaps by Rosaria Quartararo's *Roma tra Londra e Berlino* (1980), argues that Mussolini, far from committing himself unreservedly to Nazi Germany, had in mind an "equidistant" position between the power blocs. But if this indeed was his intention, he proved quite incapable of sustaining it.

Whereas the Duce's extra-European aspirations ineluctably cut him off from the western democracies, events on the Continent were soon to transform the Axis into an obligation for Fascist Italy from which there was no escape.

The catalyst was the union of Austria with Nazi Germany. During 1937, Mussolini came around to accepting the *Anschluss* which earlier he had done as much as anyone to prevent. The Germans were skillfully insistent in conveying that the price for a continued special Rome-Berlin relationship was *Anschluss*. Mussolini was wooed on a visit to Berlin by a spectacular display of German military might, coupled with repeated pledges to respect Italian sovereignty over the Alto Adige. Gradually, the negative expostulations with which Italian Fascist leaders were wont to greet any mention of *Anschluss* died away. In November 1937, the Nazi foreign minister, Ribbentrop, visited Rome, tested the waters, and returned to Berlin convinced that Germany now had a free hand in Austria. When Hitler did move on Austria the following March, he gave Mussolini only twelve hours notice. But this did not disturb Mussolini. "The Duce accepted the whole thing in a very friendly manner," Hitler was informed. "He sends you his regards." Responded the Führer: "Please tell Mussolini that I shall never forget him for this."

The beginning of the end of Fascist Italy can be dated from the *Anschluss* of March 13, 1938. The shadow of the predatory and overwhelming force of Pan-Germanism fell over Italy. Not only did the Italian hold on the Alto Adige appear threatened, but also Italy's very integrity; in process was the transformation of Fascist Italy into a satellite of Nazi Germany. Evidence of this was clearly visible to the Italian people. For example, it was announced that the Italian army was to march to a new *passo romano,* which turned out to be indistinguishable from the German goose step. More seriously, in July 1938, a Manifesto of the Race heralded the introduction into Italy of anti-Semitic measures which bore a distinct resemblance to the Nazi Nuremberg Laws. This development was a shock. Italian Fascism, while containing a small hard core of racists, had hitherto shunned anti-Semitism. Mussolini himself apparently believed in the existence of a Jewish world-wide conspiracy, but he was also known to have been scathing about Hitler's obsession with the Jews and to have encouraged Zionism as a means of disrupting the British Empire. Furthermore, as late as 1934, an attempt to promote a fascist international had foundered on the clash between Italy's corporativist Fascists and anti-Semitic national socialists from the Balkans. Mussolini was at pains to stress Italian Fascism's new racist theory was its own, not a Nazi German import, and in truth the Manifesto of the Race was built on racist antecedents in Italy's colonies. Yet, its coincidental timing with the blossoming of the Rome-Berlin Axis is too obvious to overlook. The issue is summed up by Meir Michaelis in his magisterial *Mussolini and the Jews* (1978):

> That Italian Fascism arrived at "some form of racial doctrine" independently of German influence is perfectly true; for the ban on miscegenation in Africa was decreed before the birth of the Axis. It is equally true, however, that this doctrine did not take on an anti-Jewish character until Italy became a pawn of the Reich.

Because these anti-Semitic laws seemed alien both to Italy and to Fascism, many Italians, including P.N.F. officials, to their eternal credit, did their best to circumvent them. Mussolini's undeniable subservience to Hitler cost him dear; the popular euphoria of the Ethiopian war was replaced within two years by a resigned cynicism. After 1938, Mussolini's popularity went into an unrelieved decline.

On the international stage, Mussolini's parody of Hitlerian policy appeared even more marked. He mimicked the Führer's revisionist demands in eastern Europe by raising an Italian irredentist cry for the French territory of Nice, Corsica, and Tunisia. In April 1939, a few weeks after the Nazis dismantled Czechoslovakia, Fascist Italy kept pace by invading and annexing Albania—although Albania had been a virtual Italian protectorate for more than a decade. Mussolini's efforts to recoup prestige abroad received little assistance from Hitler. On the contrary, the Führer, once he was certain of Fascist Italy's dependence on Germany, showed little regard for Mussolini's susceptibilities. "The brutal friendship," in F. W. Deakin's apt phrase, was inaugurated. Despite protestations to consult Mussolini at every turn, Hitler never did so. "Whenever Hitler moves he sends me a telegram," the Duce would grumble. Although resentful of the servile position into which he had fallen, Mussolini was also dazzled by German power. Thus, he convinced himself that association with the strongest state on the Continent added to Fascist Italy's stature.

Given Fascist Italy's inability to break with Nazi Germany, it was almost inevitable that sooner or later the generic Rome-Berlin Axis would be converted into a formal alliance. Indeed, in the aftermath of the *Anschluss,* Ciano and Ribbentrop tried unsuccessfully to reach an agreement. However, events during the rest of 1938 determined that the effort would be resumed. In September, the Munich Conference took place, and Hitler let it be understood that it was an appeal by Mussolini which had persuaded him to go to the conference table instead of the battlefield. For a brief moment, Mussolini basked in his role of *arbiter mundi.* But once in Munich, he was completely overshadowed by the Führer. The granting of all Hitler's demands on Czechoslovakia confirmed Mussolini's impression of irresistible Nazi strength and the feebleness of the western democracies. The Duce left Munich more determined than ever to swim with the tide.

In the new year 1939, he took up a Nazi German proposal, made some weeks earlier, to transform the Anti-Comintern Pact of Germany, Italy, and Japan into a triple alliance. But the Japanese, after several weeks of negotiation, balked; whereupon Mussolini proposed a simple Italo-German alliance. With incredible nonchalance, Mussolini left the drafting to the Germans, who reproduced essentially the same text that Italy had rejected the previous year. "I have never read such a pact," wrote Ciano in his diary. "It contains some real dynamite." Most notably, article III scorned the diplomatic convention that military alliances should operate for defensive purposes only. This was an offensive pact; if either party became involved in war for whatever cause, the other was obliged to lend support "with all its military forces on land, on sea, and in the air." Ciano, who traveled to Berlin to conclude the accord, made it clear that Fascist Italy would not be ready for war until 1943. Ribbentrop assured him that Germany, too, had no intention of provoking a conflict before that date. With this private understanding, the alliance was signed on May 22, 1939.

The treaty was shortly named the Pact of Steel (after Mussolini's initial suggestion of a "pact of blood" was quashed.) It brought the wheel of Italian history almost full circle, for the Duce's diplomatic path was one which Italy had explored before. Liberal Italy, like Fascist Italy, had once turned against the western powers—and for a similar sort of imperial reason. In 1881, Italy fell into dispute with France over Tunisia; in 1935, Mussolini quarreled with Britain over Ethiopia. In both eras, the Italian reaction was the same: flight into the arms of the ascendant continental power, Germany. In 1882, Italy signed the Triple Alliance (which was renewed on several occasions, for the last time in 1911); in May 1939, Italy pledged herself in the Pact of Steel. The commitment of liberal Italy to imperial Germany in 1914 was in every way less than that of Mussolini's Italy to Nazi Germany in 1939. Nonetheless, on the outbreak of both the world wars, Italy was at least formally a German ally.

6
War

In the last week of August 1939, it became clear that Hitler's designs on Danzig and the Polish Corridor were about to embroil him in a war with Britain and France. This faced Mussolini with a disagreeable choice: either to honor Italy's signature on the Pact of Steel before he was ready for war, or else to repeat history still further by imitating Italy's neutrality of 1914. Mussolini found himself urged on all sides to stay out of war. Ciano had suddenly grown disenchanted with the Axis he had helped to form, and although confining his most barbed comments on the Nazis to his diary, he now spoke out for caution and neutrality. From Berlin, Attolico warned of German untrustworthiness, and the Nazi-Soviet nonaggression pact, concluded on August 23 without prior notice to Italy, seemed to bear out his words. But what counted most with Mussolini was the unequivocal opinion of the general staff that Italy was completely unprepared for war. Fascist Italy had asserted this very point in signing the Pact of Steel, so it provided a credible excuse to avoid fulfilling the treaty three months later. To clinch the argument, Attolico was authorized on August 26 to present to the German government a statement of what Italy needed from Germany in order to undertake war. It included a formidable list of raw materials, headed by coal (six million tons required) and steel (two million tons). For good measure, Italy also asked for 150 antiaircraft batteries with ammunition. "Enough to kill a bull—if a bull could read," quipped Ciano. Attolico on his own initiative added the impossible stipulation that the supplies be delivered before the outbreak of hostilities. Hitler recognized Italy's demands as tantamount to a declaration of neutrality. On the 27th, he released Mussolini from his obligations under the Pact of Steel, asking the Duce only "to support my struggle psychologically with your press or . . . by demonstrative military measures, to compel Britain and France at least to tie down some of their forces, or at any rate to leave them in uncertainty." In a last-ditch attempt to assert himself, Mussolini offered his services as mediator between the Nazis and the Anglo-French. But neither side showed much enthusiasm for this. Thus, there was no alternative to Italian neutrality—or as Mussolini preferred to call it, nonbelligerency—when, on September 3, Britain and France declared war on Germany.

Neutrality in Mussolini's eyes was an ignominious posture. No matter how benevolently neutrality might be exercised in Germany's favor, Fascist Italy had deserted Germany just as liberal Italy had done in 1914. This comparison galled Mussolini, who conveniently overlooked his own part in Italy's switch to the Anglo-French camp during the First World War. And the relief with which neutrality was greeted by the mass of Italians infuriated him more. "The Italian race is a nation of sheep," he sneered. National honor, it appeared, could only be redeemed by intervention. From the new year 1940, Mussolini began to speak of his determination to intervene at the earliest advantageous moment. No amount of argument or pressure could deter him. Ciano, now decidedly anti-German and anti-interventionist, was powerless. King Victor Emmanuel, still clinging to his constitutional powers in matters of peace and war, tried in vain to sway Mussolini. The papacy was openly and consistently in favor of continued Italian neutrality. The American President Roosevelt sent Sumner Welles to Europe on a peace mission; while in Rome, Welles urged the Duce to stay out of the war. The British and French used less friendly persuasion; their partial blockade of the Mediterranean offered a taste of what might befall Italy if she became a belligerent. But when the moment for which Mussolini was waiting arrived, he was unshaken in his warlike resolve.

The Nazi blitzkrieg of May 1940 swept over the Low Countries and into northern France. The prospect of Germany's proximate conquest of France and conceivable victory over Britain persuaded Mussolini that he must act at once if he were not to miss the spoils of war. On June 10, Italy declared war on Britain and France. From the balcony of the Palazzo Venezia the Duce announced:

> We are entering the lists against the plutocratic and reactionary democracies of the west, which have always hindered the advance and often plotted against the very existence of the Italian people. . . . According to the laws of fascist morality, when one has a friend, one goes with him to the very end. We have done this and will do this with Germany, with her people, with her victorious armed forces.

The French ambassador told Ciano: "The Germans are hard masters. You too will learn this." Ciano told his diary: "I am sad, very sad. The adventure begins. May God help Italy."

Fascist Italy was no more ready for war in 1940 than in the Munich and Danzig crises when Mussolini had reluctantly admitted the fact. The Duce's declaration of war was thus fraught with risk, even allowing for France's exhaustion. Unless the government in London could also be forced into quick surrender, Italy and her empire were vulnerable to British naval power. Yet, in the summer of 1940, Mussolini actually hoped for continued warfare, arguing that the more fighting Italy engaged in, the greater would be her bargaining power in the ultimate peace settlement. In this eagerness to put Italy's suspect war machine to the test may lie a hint that Mussolini had reversed his former priorities in domestic and foreign politics. Rather than a radical reformation of Italian society at home paving the way for conquest abroad, perhaps war itself would now spark a real Fascist revolution within Italy—an echo of Mussolini's syndicalist case for intervention in 1915. MacGregor Knox, who endorses this view in his *Mussolini Unleashed* (1982), holds that "Mussolini's war was to be a war of internal as well as foreign conquest, a war of revenge on the Italian establishment." But in addition, Mussolini's rash plunge into the Second World War betokened a deep-seated preference for his own propaganda over the truth. Mack Smith describes Mussolini as "an artist in propaganda," but also calls him gullible. The inference is that the Duce became so adept at peddling false images that he ended up selling them to himself. Certainly, his actions in 1940 are inexplicable save in terms of a blind trust in Fascist Italy's military prowess, autarchy, and Social Darwinian inevitability.

It was soon clear that Mussolini had miscalculated. For four days Italy waged an offensive in the Alps against a French foe so catastrophically defeated in the north that it had already sued Germany for an armistice. In spite of their superior numbers, the Italians were able to advance only a few miles in one or two sectors of the front. Mussolini was thus in no position to make demands at the negotiating table. Furthermore, it was imperative that the Axis keep French North Africa, and the French naval squadrons there, neutral and out of British hands. The price of ensuring this was restraint in dealing with defeated France. Hence, Hitler tolerated the semiautonomous Vichy regime in the south of France, while Mussolini reduced his claims to a few square miles of Alpine territory and demilitarization of Franco-Italian frontiers. For Fascist Italy it was a paltry reward for intervention.

This disappointment led directly to Mussolini's next adventure. His first thought was to find compensation elsewhere, and his gaze turned to the Balkans. As usual, a move by Mussolini followed one by Hitler. In early October, Germany occupied Rumania for her oil wells. Mussolini decided to pay back Hitler in his own coin. "He will find out from the papers that I have occupied Greece," the Duce confided to Ciano. On October 28, the Führer arrived in Florence for a conference to find that Mussolini had presented him with the *fait accompli* of a Greek invasion. But Mussolini's "parallel war" soon came to grief. The Italian armies were swiftly and ingloriously pushed back across the Albanian border. The Germans, partly to save Axis face and partly to further their own Balkan ambitions, came to Italy's aid. In the spring of 1941, practically the entire Balkan peninsula fell under German control. Save in Albania and a small part of Yugoslav Croatia, Italian influence was virtually excluded.

German grand strategy called for the Italian war effort to concentrate on the Mediterranean and North Africa. Here Italy enjoyed some success at the outset. In September 1940, the Italian army in Libya crossed the Egyptian border and advanced sixty miles toward Suez. But this proved to be a strategic British retreat. In December, the Italians were in full flight westwards. At the same time, the British began to capture Italy's East African empire. By May 1941, Ethiopia, for which Mussolini had staked so much a bare six years earlier, was lost to Italy forever. Meanwhile, what happened in the Balkans happened also in Africa: the Germans took over. Although the main North African campaign remained nominally an Italian operation, troops and supplies came increasingly from Germany. Most important, effective command passed to the German General Rommel.

Nor was this all. Because Italy was the natural conduit for war matériel to the African and Mediterranean theaters, the peninsula was quickly infiltrated by a horde of German officials. To assure Axis control over the narrow waist of the Mediterranean, the German air force was summoned after the main Italian fleet was crippled by a British air raid in November 1940. Thus, the Luftwaffe established itself securely in Sicily and southern Italy. To all intents, the German occupation of Italy started in the winter of 1940–1941.

The successive military defeats—in the Alps, the Balkans, the Mediterranean, and Africa—exposed with startling suddenness the sham of Italian Fascism. Mussolini had not magically transformed Italy into a major power. Tourist trains might run on time, but the "eight million bayonets" and the planes "so numerous that they could blot out the sun," of which Mussolini had boasted, were fictional. In 1940, Fascist Italy mobilized 1.63 million men and equipped them with a rifle modeled in 1891 and artillery of a First World War design. The air force had only about 1,000 planes fit to fly and a chronic shortage of fuel. The navy alone approached a state of readiness, although it accomplished little when put to the test.

Autarchy was an equally empty boast. Cut off from her normal sources of supply, Italy turned to Germany. But the Nazi regime exploited its partner shamelessly, and actually received more goods from Italy than it provided. Due to lack of imports and labor, the Italian indices of production between 1940 and 1943 declined steadily—industry by some 35 percent and agriculture by 25 percent. To pay for the war, the Fascist government raised taxes, but this was insufficient; most of the expenses were met by borrowing and note-printing. This was a prescription for inflation, which the government tried to fight by massive economic regulation. Rationing was severe, not only of luxury items but of basic foodstuffs. Between 1941 and 1943, Italy's per capita food ration was roughly equivalent to that of the Poles under Nazi occupation. Price and wage controls met with modest success, but real wages fell by over 30 percent in three years. Prices hit astronomical peaks on the black market, which was kept in a thriving condition not least by the more dishonest Fascist party hacks.

Mussolini's reaction to the rising catastrophe was to retreat still further from reality. He surrounded himself with younger Fascists whose character had been formed by Fascist education. These were obedient sycophants and professional optimists who pandered to Mussolini's vanity and self-pity. Therefore, every setback was ascribed, not to the regime's shortcomings, but to the cowardice of the Italian people who did not deserve so great a leader as the Duce. On occasion, Mussolini compared himself to Napoleon, and even Jesus. His entourage never questioned Mussolini's fantasy that an Axis victory lay just around the corner. Hitler, too, made his contribution with his endless promises of a revolutionary secret weapon in the making. Yet, although Mussolini exuded confidence in public, inwardly he was in a state of nervous tension. This caused his gastric ulcer to return, and sometimes for days on end he was in considerable pain. Mussolini had never shown a liking for the hard grind of administration. Now, when the war required all his attention, he was growing physically as well as temperamentally incapable.

The Italian state was left to drift further because of Mussolini's fatalistic streak. He had always been superstitious and was mortally afraid of *iettatori* (those who possessed the evil eye). His belief in destiny became pronounced during the war years. He claimed to have followed his star which had led him into power and into the Axis. There was no alternative, he insisted, but to continue on the road charted by providence. Of course, this happened also to be the road charted by Hitler. Verbally and in private, Mussolini grew progressively more querulous about Nazi high-handedness; but his actions belied his words. The attack on Greece was his last important initiative in foreign policy. From the beginning of 1941, he followed resignedly in Hitler's wake. On June 22, 1941, Nazi Germany invaded the Soviet Union. Mussolini immediately insisted that Italy join the campaign in order to be in at the kill. So an Italian expeditionary force was scraped together and sent to the Russian front, where it suffered cruelly. On December 7, 1941, Japan bombed Pearl Harbor. The Tripartite Pact, signed by Germany, Italy, and Japan in September 1940, was a defensive alliance; therefore, Italy was under no obligation to enter a Japanese-American war. Moreover, in the past Mussolini had warned Hitler against underestimating American power. Nevertheless, on December 11, Nazi Germany and Fascist Italy jointly declared war on the United States.

It was plain that as long as Mussolini continued in power, Fascist Italy would remain loyal to the Axis. Nearly twenty years of *ducismo*, or Duce-worship, had trained Italians to accept Mussolini's policies, no matter what misery they might bring. However, there is always a breaking point, and it was reached in Italy in 1943. By this juncture, living conditions were abysmal. In addition to the rationing of food and clothing, there was a ban on the sale of silk, cotton, and leather goods. Metal objects ranging from kitchenware to statuary were requisitioned. Public transport was curtailed, as was the use of electricity; in Rome, street lights were switched off on moonlit nights. Popular discontent came to the surface in March 1943 in a series of strikes in Turin and Milan. These were the first serious working-class demonstrations in Italy since 1922, and the first against the Axis war effort anywhere in Europe. A leaflet widely distributed among the strikers called for "bread, peace, and freedom." the regime restored calm temporarily by granting wage increases, but the political overtones of the strikes were ominous for Fascism's future.

The real impetus for change, however, was a galloping deterioration of the military situation. In November 1942, the British cracked the Axis front at El Alamein in Egypt. Rommel's Italo-German army was compelled to retreat steadily westwards. Also in November, Anglo-American forces landed in French Morocco and Algeria, and started to move east. Rommel was trapped in an Allied pincer movement. Mussolini timidly suggested to Hitler that he negotiate an armistice in Russia (where the Red army had checked the Nazi advance at Stalingrad) in order to concentrate on the danger in North Africa. But the Führer would not hear of this. In May 1943, the Axis forces were overwhelmed in Tunisia; 200,000 men were killed, wounded, or captured. The Allies were then poised to strike across the Mediterranean narrows. On July 9, they landed in Sicily; in less than a week the island was taken. It was only a matter of time before the Allies invaded mainland Italy. In the meanwhile, Rome was given its initial taste of aerial bombardment.

Against this background, a coherent opposition to Mussolini took shape in the first half of 1943. It was a movement motivated almost exclusively by dislike of the Axis and the war of which Mussolini was the symbol. To change the direction of Italian policy it was necessary first to bring Mussolini to heel, or else to remove him altogether. To downgrade or overthrow the Duce was to imperil the entire Fascist regime, but this was only marginally an opposition to Fascism itself, the principal actors being either Fascists themselves or fellow travelers of long standing. The two focal points of opposition lay in the royal palace and within the Fascist party.

Relations between King Victor Emmanuel and Mussolini were always formally correct, but in reality there was no love lost be-

tween them. The king had admired Mussolini in the early days of
Fascism and helped to save him in the Matteotti crisis. But disenchantment came with the Fascist erosion of the royal prerogative. In
1928, the Fascist Grand Council was given cognizance of all constitutional questions, including even the succession to the throne.
Ten years later, Mussolini invented a new title, "marshal of the
empire," for both duce and king. Victor Emmanuel suspected that
this usurped his constitutional command of the armed forces, and
complained strenuously that he and Mussolini were put on the same
level. In fact, it was Mussolini's objective to create just such a
dyarchy. After 1940, the king's resentment increased the more
the Duce arrogated to himself direction of the war effort. By 1943,
he was glad to have an excuse to take action against Mussolini.
Through the minister of the royal household, the Duke d'Acquarone, contact was made with other disaffected elements. Some
of these, like Ivanoe Bonomi, were retired politicians of the pre-
Fascist era; others were dissident Fascists.

Discontent within the Fascist party might not have crystallized
as it did but for Mussolini's comprehensive changing of the guard in
February 1943. Among other changes, the prominent hierarchs,
Ciano, Grandi, and Bottai, were dismissed from their respective
ministries of foreign affairs, justice, and education. Afterwards,
these three were the nucleus of Fascist opposition to Mussolini. The
malcontents' strategy was to use the party apparatus to overcome
Mussolini, rather in the way that the party consuls had seemed to
dictate to Mussolini in the closing stages of the Matteotti affair. For
this purpose, they advocated the convocation of the Grand Council
of Fascism, which Mussolini had not summoned into session since
December 1939. On July 16, 1943, a deputation of fifteen, led by
the party secretary, Carlo Scorza, waited on Mussolini. Grandi and
Ciano were absent although there in spirit. Bottai and Farinacci, the
latter one of the consuls of 1924, were the spokesmen. They asked
for a meeting of the Grand Council, and Mussolini grudgingly
complied.

On July 20, Mussolini returned from another encounter with

Hitler, this one at Feltre north of Venice. Hitler had fed Mussolini the usual diet of promises of aid and ultimate victory. Everyone knew that once more the Duce had failed to stand up to the Führer. Grandi seized the opportunity to draw up a motion for submission to the Fascist Grand Council. It called for the reactivation of the legal organs of the Fascist state—the Grand Council itself, the Council of Ministers, parliament, and the corporations. It also proposed that the king resume sole command of the armed forces. Grandi began to canvass support for his motion among the members of the Grand Council. To avoid any charge of treason, he even disclosed it to Mussolini, who apparently did not grasp its thrust and took it calmly. Nonetheless, Grandi was uneasy. When the Grand Council met in the evening of the 24th, he carried two grenades with him into the Palazzo Venezia.

Several first-hand accounts of this fateful session exist, notably one by Mussolini and another by Grandi. They do not tally, but enough is clear. The Duce defended his foreign policy at length. He refuted slurs on the Axis by citing figures of war matériel that Italy had received from Nazi Germany. He sought to justify his own military record by making a great deal of an inconsequential Italian victory at the Mediterranean island of Pantelleria in June 1942. The discussion which followed was disjointed and confused. Tempers flared occasionally. Grandi spoke for his resolution, and Bottai and Ciano backed him briefly. Farinacci and Scorza tried unsuccessfully to introduce resolutions of their own. There was an intermission of fifteen minutes, during which Guido Buffarini, one of the Petacci clan, privately urged Mussolini to arrest Grandi and his followers. But Mussolini, who seemed in the course of the proceedings to have grown more detached than angry, refused. The conference resumed. Ultimately, after more than nine hours of random talk, Grandi's motion was voted on. It was carried by a majority of nineteen to seven.

By itself, the Grand Council's decision might not have altered much, which was doubtless why Mussolini tolerated it with relatively good grace. However, it was at this point that the royal plot dovetailed with the party attack on Mussolini—as some of the dissidents perhaps hoped and expected. Since Mussolini's return from Feltre, the king had decided to dismiss him. Hearing of the Grand Council's vote, he realized that the moment had come. Mussolini, for his part, completely misread the situation, and blithely assumed that he still had the king's support. The morning after the Grand Council session, he telephoned to ask for an audience with the king that afternoon—just as he had done routinely for over twenty years in order to report to the monarch. The rest of the day he spent in his office. At 5 P.M. on July 25, he was driven unsuspecting to the Villa Savoia.

Once closeted with the king, Mussolini launched into a report of the military situation. He then turned to the events in the Grand Council, which he described as a purely consultative body. But here Victor Emmanuel interrupted him and requested his resignation. A new government was planned under Marshal Badoglio, who ironically had received his field marshal's baton for his part in Mussolini's conquest of Ethiopia. The Duce tried to argue, and the king was overheard to say: "I am sorry, I am sorry, but the solution could not have been otherwise." When the stunned Mussolini emerged from the villa, he found that D'Acquarone had made certain arrangements for him. He was approached by a *Carabiniere* officer who told him: "His Majesty has charged me with the protection of your person." Whereupon, he was efficiently whisked off to prison in an ambulance. As news of Mussolini's downfall spread, there was shouting in the streets—mostly in celebration. Nowhere was there the slightest sign of a Fascist insurrection—eloquent testimony to the final bankruptcy of the Fascist movement.

7

An Epilogue

The Badoglio ministry, although composed of men who had once accepted Mussolini without much qualm, was anxious to avoid the stigma of Fascism. It called itself a government of technicians and sought to liquidate the consequences of Mussolini's foreign policy. Most Italians would doubtless have preferred to get out of the Second World War altogether. But events soon ruled out a resumption of neutrality. In late August 1943, after several weeks of confusion, the Badoglio government embarked on serious negotiations with the Allies. On September 3, an armistice was concluded at Cassibile in Sicily. Italy's surrender was announced to the world five days later. By prearrangement, Anglo-American forces landed immediately on mainland Italy—in Calabria on September 3 and near Salerno on the 8th. The Germans had anticipated Italy's desertion and been given time to prepare for it. They occupied Rome on the 11th and swiftly extended their sway over all the Italian peninsula north of the battlefront. Victor Emmanuel and his ministers fled south and took refuge with the Allies. On October 13, the Badoglio government declared war on Germany. By this expression of cobelligerency with the Allies, royalist Italy hoped to revert to the position of 1915–1918.

In the meantime, the possession of Mussolini's person had proved an embarrassment to the Badoglio regime. The former Duce, who was ill and tired, would have liked nothing better than to retire to private life in his native Romagna. But he was far too notorious for this. For one thing, the Nazis wanted to use him to keep as many Italians as possible loyal to the Axis. To prevent Mussolini falling into German hands, the Badoglio authorities refused to divulge his whereabouts, and moved him rapidly from one place of confinement to another. Finally, however, the Germans caught up with him at Gran Sasso, a mountain resort in the Apennines. A daring rescue by glider was executed on September 12; Mussolini's jailers, bewildered by the Cassibile armistice and the threatened Nazi takeover of Italy, put up no resistance to speak of. Mussolini was taken to Munich where he was reunited with his family. Then he traveled to East Prussia to see Hitler, who told him that he should return to German-occupied Italy to head a new Fascist regime. Mussolini was not enthusiastic, but he agreed nevertheless. In a sense, this was a patriotic gesture, for he hoped that his presence in Italy might stand between the full force of Nazi tyranny and the Italian people.

Hitler also imposed a German doctor on Mussolini. Considering the Führer's predilection for medical quacks, Mussolini was lucky that Dr. Zachariae proved to be thoroughly competent. He treated Mussolini for anemia and an enlarged liver, and within weeks a noticeable change for the better occurred. Yet withal, Mussolini, who had just passed his sixtieth birthday, appeared an old man. The characteristic fire and vigor were almost gone. He was now a stolid figure who moved with deliberation. His eyesight, too, had grown very weak, and he could read only with strong glasses and electric light.

Since King Victor Emmanuel had renounced Fascism, Mussolini's new regime was perforce republican—the Italian Social Republic officially. Its headquarters, chosen by the Germans, lay along the left bank of Lake Garda, some hundred miles south of the Brenner Pass. Mussolini's home and office were situated in Gargnano. The administrative offices were scattered among several towns and villages, some of the more important in the small town of Salò. In fact, the regime has gone down in history as the Salò Republic.

Those who followed Mussolini on his last political odyssey comprised a nondescript company. Of his very few personal intimates, his family and also Clara Petacci remained loyal. By contrast, most of his erstwhile political cronies, the Fascist hierarchs, had cut themselves off by their stand in the Grand Council session of July 24–25. Consequently, the principal offices in Mussolini's new government were filled by comparatively unknown Fascists. Alessandro Pavolini became party secretary, Buffarini minister of the interior, Fernando Mezzasomma minister of popular culture, and Angelo Tarchi minister of corporate economy. Mussolini himself took over the foreign ministry, chiefly because no one else of sufficient stature could be found; a career diplomat, Count Mazzolini, served as his undersecretary.

Many of the Salò Fascists nursed an extreme vindictiveness against those who had voted against Mussolini in the Grand Council. Sparked by Pavolini, the demand was raised for punishment of the "criminals of July 25." The main target was Ciano who, trusting for protection in his special relationship with Mussolini, had joined the latter in Munich. The Nazis, well aware of Ciano's anti-German opinions, kept him under surveillance in Munich after Mussolini's return to Italy. In due course, they were delighted to turn him over to his enemies in the Salò Republic for trial. As for Mussolini, he harbored little or no rancor toward Ciano and the other hierarchs who had crossed him. But he yielded to the importunities of the Pavolini faction and the Germans, and a special tribunal was established at Verona.

The Verona trial was a travesty. Only six of those who had voted for Grandi's motion could be apprehended and charged with treason. Ciano and Marshal De Bono, one of the quadrumvirate which had directed the March on Rome in 1922, were the only notable Fascists. During the trial the prosecution made much of a conspiracy against the Duce. No proof was adduced, and the supposed plot was never precisely established. Nevertheless, all the prisoners were found guilty. Five of them, including Ciano and De Bono, received the death sentence.

Edda Ciano tried to save her husband's life by offering in exchange certain of his papers, and above all his diary with its revelations of Axis diplomacy. Mussolini, although upset by the persecution of his son-in-law, rejected the bargain and washed his hands of the entire Verona affair. The breach with Edda, who had always been his favorite child, was never healed. The Germans seemed more eager to obtain the compromising diary until Hitler personally ordered that negotiations with Edda Ciano be broken off. Leaving behind final appeals to Mussolini and Hitler, she made her way safely into Switzerland, carrying the diary with her. (Published after the war, it has proved an invaluable source of information on Fascist diplomacy between 1936 and 1943.) No reprieve being granted Ciano and his four condemned colleagues, they were executed in Verona on January 11, 1944, by a Fascist firing squad. In the wings waited a German S.S. detachment, lest the Italians prove unequal to the task.

Odious though it was, the bloodletting at Verona represented the sole occasion on which the Salò regime was able to assert itself unequivocally. At every other turn, it was frustrated by the Germans. It was no accident that the Fascist administration was housed far from Rome, nor that Mussolini never again set foot in the Italian capital (although it was not captured by the Allies until June 1944.) These things were symptomatic of the basic truth about the Salò Republic, namely, that it was not a genuine Italian government at all. No matter how much Mussolini intended to intercede for the Italians, he was from 1943 to 1945 totally a German puppet.

Everywhere Nazi officials issued orders without reference to the Salò authorities. The German Ministry of Labor arbitrarily conscripted Italians for war work. In October 1943, Berlin declared the whole of northern Italy to be subject to German military government. What rankled most, however, was German conduct in the Alto Adige and the other territories which Italy had inherited from the Habsburg Empire in 1918. On the heels of the Pact of Steel in 1939, Nazi Germany had formally reaffirmed Italian sovereignty over the Alto Adige. In addition, an agreement had been reached to resettle in Austria and Bavaria as many Germans as were willing to leave the Alto Adige. But by 1943, less than 80,000 out of 200,000 had been relocated. Then, the events of the summer and fall of 1943 gave Hitler an excuse to renege on past engagements. In the Alto Adige and other ex-Austrian lands, German *Gauleiters* were appointed; Italian prefects were kept virtually incommunicado with Salò; and Italian troops were disarmed and interned. Mussolini tried to extract from Berlin a definition of the status of these areas. None was forthcoming. Yet, it was plain that their *de facto* annexation to the Third Reich had already taken place. The situation has been neatly summated, with a nod in the direction of Hitler's Austrian roots, in the phrase "the Habsburg revenge."

Mussolini recognized that a humiliating subservience to Nazi Germany was inevitable unless the Salò regime could mount a credible war effort of its own. This required the cooperation of all Italians within the jurisdiction of Salò. To cultivate such mass allegiance, Mussolini tried to reconvert Fascism into what it had been at the outset in 1919—a radical, populist movement. Sheer opportunism can never be ruled out in any Mussolinian decision, but he may not have been altogether insincere in this latest shift. He had delayed his renunciation of republicanism in 1922 as long as he dared. As late as 1924, he had still been hinting at reconciliation with the socialists—and through them with Italy's working-class. Nor should one imagine that his marriage of convenience with the Italian establishment had exorcised his youthful resentment of those born with privilege; they had no place in his ideal Fascist society. So it was not totally out of character when he announced that the Salò Republic would pursue a moderate socialist economic policy. In particular, workers were to have more say in the management of factories, while the industries most vital to the war effort were to be nationalized. But once again, German officials in northern Italy intervened, systematically sabotaging all efforts to change the status quo. Moreover, the Italian workers, after more than twenty years of Fascist collusion with the capitalists, remained understandably skeptical of Mussolini's rediscovered socialism.

The Italian people, far from rallying to Mussolini, showed a distinct preference for the resistance movement, a spontaneous popular uprising against the Nazi occupation of most of Italy and against the Salò Republic as the Germans' accomplice. Because of Fascist Italian defeats on the battlefield, the view that Italy was a nation of cowards had increased in currency. Even Mussolini had helped to spread the notion to excuse his own failings. The resistance proved effectively that Italians could fight as bravely as any other people if they felt the cause was worthwhile; obviously Fascism had not been considered worth dying for. Some factions were more to the fore than others in the resistance. The P.C.I., with an underground network already in place from the Fascist era, provided an invaluable organizational framework, and individual communists spurred by ideological conviction proved uncommonly willing to risk their lives in the anti-Fascist cause. Next in importance was the *Partito d'Azione* (Action Party), a coalition of "liberal socialists" created by the *fuorusciti* in exile and destined to form the first, brief post–Second World War government in Italy. The foot-soldiers of the resistance were drawn in the main from the factory proletariat and the peasantry, understandably since these classes had borne the brunt of Fascist economic mismanagement and compromise with propertied interests. But more important than special contributions was the fact that all conditions of Italians and shades of opinion, save Fascism, came together in the resistance. As a national effort, it earned, in memory of the kindling of the Italian spirit which preceded unification, the title of the second *risorgimento*. For a short while, it gave rise to an integration of Italian society of the sort that Mussolini had tried for twenty years to impose; mockingly, it was accomplished at his expense.

Scorned by the Nazis and the majority of Italians alike, Mussolini passed a miserable year and a half on the shores of Lake Garda; he disliked lakes and their winter mists. His office hours were spent in pointless paperwork. Occasionally, he gave a speech over the radio. In December 1944, he made several appearances in Milan, where he was greeted with acclaim. However, his audiences were hardly representative of Italian opinion at large, and some were palpably hand-picked.

From the new year 1945, it was just a question of waiting for the end. By April, Allied troops were about to overrun the Po Valley, much of which was already controlled by the partisans of the resistance movement. On April 20, Mussolini moved to Milan, resolved to seek an armistice with either the Allies or the partisans, or both. Archbishop Schuster of Milan, whose main concern was to spare his city a siege, acted as one intermediary. On the 25th, the archbishop succeeded in bringing Mussolini face to face with representatives of the political arm of the resistance, the *Comitati di liberazione nazionale* (C.L.N.). The C.L.N. offered the Salò regime only unconditional surrender. Mussolini seemed ready to capitulate. But when he learned that the German command in Italy, behind his back, had also been negotiating with the Allies for a separate armistice, he suspected a trick. Breaking off the talks with the C.L.N., he decided to flee posthaste to the mountains north of Milan. His idea was not so much to make a stand there but merely to delay the day of reckoning.

Mussolini left carrying his most private papers in two briefcases; these included his correspondence with Hitler, later published, although it is not certain that all these "handbag files" have seen the light of day. He was accompanied by a score of Fascists and a German escort. Pavolini stayed in Milan to assemble as many blackshirts as possible and then follow Mussolini. Mussolini and his entourage wasted the 26th in and around Como, waiting for Pavolini's column which never did catch up. Fearful of an attack by partisans, at dawn on the 27th, Mussolini's group joined for protection a German antiaircraft unit on its way to the Austrian Tyrol. Near Dongo, the convoy encountered the partisans. The latter were not strong enough to overwhelm the German force, but the Germans in their anxiety to get home before the war ended had no stomach for even a skirmish. So a deal was struck. The Germans could proceed unmolested after a search for Italian personnel.

Possibly the partisans suspected Mussolini's presence. At any rate, they found him disguised in a German greatcoat and huddled in the corner of a truck.

When the news of Mussolini's capture reached the C.L.N. in Milan, the communists wanted a summary execution. No clear decision on Mussolini's fate was taken, but a communist member of the C.L.N., who went by the name Colonel Valerio (his real name was Walter Audisio), was sent to bring Mussolini back to Milan. Neither the colonel nor the Milanese communists, however, intended that he be brought back alive. In the afternoon of April 28, Valerio traced Mussolini to a farmhouse. There, the Dongo partisans had secreted their prize, and Clara Petacci who had begged to stay with her lover, in order to forestall a rescue. Indeed, Valerio told Mussolini that he had come to rescue him. But Mussolini appeared to care little. He and Clara passively accompanied Valerio and two local partisans in a car which sped off ostensibly for Milan. About a mile along the road, Valerio stopped the car and ordered Mussolini and his mistress to stand against the stone wall surrounding a nearby villa. They were killed immediately by a burst of machine-gun fire. The next day their bodies, along with those of several other executed Fascists, were hung upside down from the roof of a gasoline station in Milan's Piazzale Loreto, the site of a notorious execution of fifteen Italian hostages ordered by the Nazis in reprisal for partisan activity. Thus, to the end Mussolini was haunted by the folly of his liaison with Hitler.

Conclusion

The significance of the Fascist era in Italian history is difficult to estimate. On the one hand, the mental scars left behind are far from healed yet; two generations after the Second World War, Fascism is still an analogue by which much in Italian life and politics is judged. This, of course, will pass away with time. In material terms, on the other hand, Fascism's legacy has already proved meager, for Mussolini's regime specialized in gestures but was always short on performance. Mussolini bequeathed an attenuated Fascist party, known today as the *Movimento sociale italiano;* some pretentious architecture of neoclassic design; and a few, too few, public works. Of more consequence, the Lateran Accords of 1929 were written into the postwar Italian constitution, and something of the corporative habit of labor negotiations also survived the war. But then, it might be argued, a reconciliation of church and state and an association of big business and big labor are inevitable twentieth-century developments; Fascism at most hastened their coming in Italy.

Fundamentally, Fascism hardly affected Italy's economic and social structure at all. True, the Italian monarchy, because of its collusion with Fascism, was abolished by popular referendum in 1946; but this was an inadvertent result of Fascism. Much more important than the institutional question, however, the traditional propertied classes did not forfeit their position under Fascism. If anything, the *latifondisti*, the rich agrarians of the Po Valley, and the industrial monopolists strengthened themselves. Some changes and innovations, of course, had been required to preserve the socioeconomic status quo. Thus, Mussolini's creation, the I.R.I., has lived on after the Second World War, but less as a regulatory agency of government than as an adjunct of the *Confindustria*. Similarly, Fascism's joint public and private ventures have continued to serve big business well; the most celebrated is probably the state petroleum agency, A.G.I.P. *(Azienda Generale Italiano Petroli)*, known to tourists by its six-legged dog trademark. Fascism, then, altered neither the distribution of wealth nor the attendant class system in Italy. Small wonder that by the time that the average Italian was called on to fight for Fascism in 1940, disillusionment had set in.

Yet, paradoxically, the lack of real accomplishment on Mussolini's part gives a clue to the kind of hold Fascism exercised over Italy for a generation. Fascism never offered a coherent political program to achieve lasting results. Instead, it served as an emotional outlet for the frustrations engendered in Italian society by the twin hydras of modern times—industrialization and nationalism. Condemning the liberal parliamentary system as incompetent to handle such problems, Italy turned by reflex action to the antithesis—Mussolini's vague authoritarianism.

On founding Fascism, Mussolini clearly hoped to ride to power on the grievances of the masses, or at least of the lower middle class. But he soon learned that a speedier way lay in pandering to the anxieties of conservatives. So Italian Fascism became for all practical purposes a right-wing movement. Early Fascist radicalism was left to be nurtured by a few middle-aged syndicalist intellectuals and a portion of Fascist youth. For Italy's conservatives, Mussolini stood as a shield against a host of evils subsumed under the headings of socialism and pacifism. It is an oversimplification, although not altogether an inaccuracy, to say that a conservative oligarchy put Mussolini in power in 1922 to protect its interests; and that when he palpably failed to do so in 1943, the same interest groups ejected him. Mussolini seemed to sense that he was used by, rather than accepted into, the Italian establishment. This imparted an extra touch of venom to his tirades against the monarchy and the pluto-crats for deserting him in 1943.

Of course, the social conditions and tensions which gave Fascism its chance in Italy were present elsewhere. Accordingly, there was considerable sympathy outside Italy for Mussolini's experiment. Admiration came not only from antibolshevik conservatives. In the English-seaking democracies, especially in the period before the Ethiopian war, many "pragmatic liberals" swallowed Mussolini's propaganda and applauded his modernizing efficiency. With the dramatic spread of fascism in the 1930s Mussolini was flattered by a measure of direct imitation. This was true in the nations on the southern and eastern periphery of Europe. There, as in Italy, the impact of the modern world on relatively backward societies bred tensions which exploded into fascism. Above all, in Catholic coun-tries the Lateran Accords and Mussolini's blueprint for a corporative state supplied a model for "clerical-corporative" regimes. Austria before the *Anschluss*, Franco's Spain, and Salazar's Portugal all owed a clear ideological debt to Fascist Italy.

Nevertheless, within a few years Fascist Italy passed from an international exemplar to a satellite of Nazi Germany. Hitler's brand of fascism, springing from an environment of modernization, was quite different in quality from the fascism of relatively backward Europe exemplified by Mussolini's movement. The Nazi harking back to a primitive, racially pure society in the past evoked little echo among Italian Fascists; the latter's rhetoric spoke of dragging their nation into the twentieth century, not of fleeing the modern age. In spite of this distinction, the sheer physical might of Ger-many determined that in the long run Nazism should achieve a hegemony over international fascism. But, in addition, Mussolini seemed to work actively and gratuitously to put his country, his movement, and himself in thrall to Hitler. This his backers could not forgive. Once his credibility as a nationalist leader was de-stroyed, the road lay open through Salò to the grisly finale at Dongo.

Bibliographical Essay

This bibliographical essay is concerned primarily with works in the English language. Certain Italian titles are included, however, either because they are of exceptional merit, or because they fill gaps in the English-language literature on Fascist Italy.

Among surveys of modern Italy, two stand out. The first of these, Denis Mack Smith's *Italy: A Modern History*, rev. ed. (Ann Arbor, 1969), is at once informative and entertaining. In mild criticism, it might be said that the *opéra bouffe* aspects of twentieth-century Italy are given too much prominence; for those Italians who lived through the Fascist era the experience was more somber than is implied here. The other notable survey is an analysis of modern Italy designed for an American audience: H. Stuart Hughes, *The United States and Italy*, 3d ed. (Cambridge, Mass., 1979). Eschewing narrative for most part, this well-written book concentrates on placing Fascism in the total context of united Italy; in this view Italy's woes in the present century have stemmed largely from the Left's failure to offer a viable governing force. On a less scholarly level is Luigi Barzini, *The Italians* (New York, 1964). This is a national character sketch written with journalistic panache and full of glittering but disputable generalizations; notwithstanding, it contains some acute historical observations. One other general title deserves mention. Shepard B. Clough, *The Economic History of Modern Italy* (New York, 1964), supplies the facts and figures of Italy's economic distress after the First World War, which helped bring Mussolini to power. Also plainly documented is the subsequent inadequacy of Fascism's economic policies.

General accounts of Fascist Italy tend to vary according to the amount of space they accord Mussolini. The standard comprehensive work, useful for reference, has long been Luigi Salvatorelli and Giovanni Mira, *Storia d'Italia nel periodo fascista*, new ed. (Turin, 1964). But a more convenient reference work for English-language readers is *A Historical Dictionary of Fascist Italy*, edited by Philip V. Cannistraro (Westport, 1982), a compendium of some 570 summary essays on specific features of the Fascist phenomenon. Among those books which relegate Mussolini to the periphery, a nice contrast is afforded by Alexander De Grand, *Italian Fascism: Its Origins and Development* (Lincoln, Neb., 1982), and Edward R. Tannenbaum, *The Fascist Experience: Italian Society and Culture* (New York, 1972). The former succinctly propounds the notion of "hyphenated fascisms" to characterize Italian Fascism's various accommodations with Italy's vested interests. It is very good on economics and the Italian class structure, but less so on political affairs. The latter is a longer work focused on education, popular culture, and the arts. The breadth of subject matter causes the treatment to fluctuate in quality, but it is a better book than many reviews allowed on its publication. Federico Chabod's *A History of Italian Fascism* (London, 1963) is a misleading title. Based on a series of interpretative lectures given at the Sorbonne in 1950, the end result is disappointingly thin and discursive. Yet it offers some sharp insights, especially into the appeal of Fascism between 1919 and 1922. In contrast, S. William Halperin, *Mussolini and Italian Fascism* (Princeton, 1964), is a title to be taken literally. In this very short but lucid survey, accompanied by some useful documentary extracts in translation, Fascism is equated with Mussolinianism. Popular works which also keep Mussolini at center stage are Giuseppe Borgese, *Goliath: The March of Fascism* (New York, 1938), and Max Gallo, *Mussolini's Italy* (New York, 1973).

Renzo De Felice's multivolume work on the Duce stands halfway between a biography and a full history of Italian Fascism; it recalls the "life and times" literary genre of a more leisurely age than our own. Unfortunately, De Felice does not write with the elegance of nineteenth-century stylists; convoluted sentences and packed detail make for hard reading and thick tomes (each one between 600 and 950 pages). The *magnum opus*, when completed, will be in four parts, with some parts divided into two volumes, as follows: 1, *Mussolini il rivoluzionario, 1883–1920*; 2, *Mussolini il fascista:* vol. I, *La conquista del potere, 1921–1925*; vol. II, *L'organizzazione dello Stato fascista, 1925–1929*; 3, *Mussolini il duce:* vol. I, *Gli anni del consenso, 1929–1936*; vol. II, *Lo Stato totalitario, 1936–1940*; 4, *Mussolini l'alleato, 1940–45* (Turin, 1965–). The final part has yet to appear. In addition, the author promises a synopsis of the whole in one volume. De Felice commands attention not just by his formidable erudition but also by the contentiousness of some of his opinions. The accusation has been made that the one has led to the other—specifically that De Felice, by immersing himself so deeply in Fascist documentary sources, has come to accept the picture conveyed therein uncritically. Hence, his acceptance of the young Mussolini as a genuine revolutionary; of an idealistic, radical strain in Fascism notionally called *fascismo-movimento;* and above all, of Fascism's consensual popular support between 1929 and 1936. In other words, say his critics, De Felice is too kind to Mussolini. Yet, his writings are not in the slightest pro-Fascist; since De Felice is a Jew who survived the Holocaust, it could hardly be otherwise. De Felice has all along insisted that his conclusions are tentative, and he has shown himself prepared to modify them. On the other hand, he has defended his positions forcefully in an interview with the American scholar, Michael A. Ledeen: *Fascism: An Informal Introduction to its Theory and Practice* (New Brunswick, 1976). Ledeen has also written an account of the storm aroused by De Felice's views in the Italy of the mid-1970s: "Renzo De Felice and the Controversy over Italian Fascism," *Journal of Contemporary History*, XI (Oct. 1976), 269–82. In sum, it may be confidently said that no serious student of Italian Fascism can afford to ignore De Felice's contribution.

In sharp contrast to the De Felice corpus is the best one-volume biography of Mussolini in English: Denis Mack Smith, *Mussolini* (London, 1982). Although packed with information, it is highly readable, and like the rest of Mack Smith's books, is straight narrative and descriptive history devoid of theorizing about Fascism or its Duce. Musslini emerges from this study a mean-spirited schemer without principles or coherent policy, skilled only in deception; it is a devastating exposé. Other single-volume works include *Mussolini: A Study in Power* (New York, 1964) by Sir Ivone Kirkpatrick who, as a British diplomat in Rome from 1930 to 1933, watched the Duce at close quarters. Predictably, he is sound on Fascist foreign policy and Mussolini's personality, but weak on domestic affairs. Also in the category of workmanlike but uneven Mussolinian biographies are those by Richard Collier and Christopher Hibbert. Laura Fermi, widow of the famous physicist who fled Fascist Italy, assays a psychological portrait in her *Mussolini* (Chicago, 1961), and does so by fixing on certain key episodes in his life. Paolo Monelli, *Mussolini: The Intimate Life of a Demagogue* (London, 1953), relates many details of the Duce's private life, including his *affaires*. A different angle is explored by Gaudens Megaro, *Mussolini in the Making* (Boston, 1938); this record of Mussolini's youth first appeared to deserved acclaim when its subject was trying to hide his leftist past. Finally worth noting, apropos Mussolini himself, is the definitive edition of his words, spoken and written: *Opera omnia di Benito Mussolini*, 44 vols., edited by Edoardo and Duilio Susmel (Florence, 1952–1963, and Rome, 1978–1980).

Biographies of individual Fascist hierarchs are not plentiful. Harry Fornari, *Mussolini's Gadfly: Roberto Farinacci* (Nashville, 1971), is barely adequate. Much more satisfactory is Alexander De Grand's *Bottai e la cultura fascista* (Rome, 1978). Badly lacking is any biography of Dino Grandi, mainly because his papers have not been accessible until recently. Sketches of fourteen hierarchs are to be found in *Uomini e volti del fascismo*, edited by Ferdinando Cordova (Rome, 1980).

The last days of liberal Italy were the seedtime of Fascism. This is the theme of a splendid and thorough survey by Christopher Seton Watson, *Italy from Liberalism to Fascism, 1870–1925* (London, 1967). A briefer treatment is Salvatore Saladino's *Italy from Unification to 1919* (Arlington Heights, Ill., 1970), a companion to this present volume in the series "Europe since 1500." The great liberal historian, Benedetto Croce, in *A History of Italy, 1870–1915* (London, 1929) presents the story of liberal Italy as mostly uninterrupted progress; it is too undiscriminating for today's taste. More balanced is A. William Salomone, *Italy in the Giolittian Era*, 2d ed. (Philadelphia, 1960), which is properly appreciative of Giolitti's problems and his shortcomings. Giolitti comes off well in Frank J. Coppa, *Planning, Protection, and Politics in Liberal Italy* (Washington, 1971), while John A. Thayer, *Italy and the Great War* (Madison, 1964), appraises without sympathy the intellectual and cultural forces which were assailing liberal Italy. The illiberal factors of imperialism and nationalism are examined by Richard A. Webster, *Industrial Imperialism, 1908–1915* (Berkeley, 1975), and R. J. B. Bosworth, *Italy: The Least of the Great Powers* (London, 1979). Webster's beat is Italian penetration of the Balkans and Asia Minor; Bosworth, though denying economic motives behind Italian expansionism, still delivers himself of a scathing, perhaps unfair, indictment of liberal Italy's diplomatic and military pursuit of *grandezza* on the eve of the First World War. The postwar fate of these nationalist aspirations is meticulously chronicled by René Albrecht-Carrié, *Italy at the Paris Peace Conference* (New York, 1938).

The circumstances surrounding the launching of the Fascist movement and its progress to absolute power are the subject of a big and impressive book by Adrian Lyttleton, *The Seizure of Power: Fascism in Italy, 1919–1929* (London, 1973). Subtlety and clarity are combined in this analysis of the factions involved, the labyrinthine route to dictatorship, and the party-state relationship. Events up to the March on Rome are presented by Angelo Tasca (pseud. Rossi), *The Rise of Italian Fascism, 1918–1922* (London, 1938). Because of the author's own communist and socialist background, the work is extremely informative on the Italian Left. For contemporary Marxist explanations of Fascism's triumph, see John M. Cammett, "Communist Theories of Fascism, 1920–1935," *Science and Society*, XXXI (1967), 149–63. A classic exposition of Fascism as a lower middle-class phenomenon remains Luigi Salvatorelli, *Nazionalfascismo* (Turin, 1923). The best regional studies of the Fascist advance are Paul Corner's *Fascism in Ferrara, 1915–1925* (London, 1975), and Anthony L. Cardoza's *Agrarian Elites and Italian Fascism: The Province of Bologna, 1901–1926* (Princeton, 1982). The Nationalists' role in breaking the ground for Fascism and in pointing the movement in a conservative direction is ably demonstrated by Alexander De Grand, *The Italian Nationalist Association* (Lincoln, Neb., 1978). The Fiume episode may be approached through the person of D'Annunzio. Michael A. Ledeen, *The First Duce: D'Annunzio at Fiume* (Baltimore, 1977), appears to go too far in claiming D'Annunzio to be the progenitor of all modern politicos who dabble in mass psychology; Anthony Rhodes, *D'Annunzio: The Poet as Superman* (London, 1959), is, despite its title, a more conventional biography.

The true nature of the Fascist dictatorship was revealed early by scholars whose work has stood the test of time remarkably well. *Mussolini's Italy* (New York, 1935; reissued, 1965) by Herman Finer is an exhaustive dissection of Mussolini's administration, which is none the less damning for its restraint. Openly polemical are the works of the *fuoruscito* historian, Gaetano Salvemini; the best-known is *Under the Axe of Fascism* (New York, 1938). Both Finer and Salvemini are critical of Mussolini's social and economic policies, and in the same vein Carl T. Schmidt, *The Corporate State in Action* (New York, 1939), examines specifically Fascist Italy's vaunted experiment and finds it sadly wanting. The famous corporative definition of Fascism, first published in *Enciclopedia italiana,* XIV (Rome, 1932), can be read in translation under the title "The Political and Social Doctrine of Fascism," *International Conciliation*, No. 306 (Jan. 1935), pp. 5–17. The background and genesis of Fascist corporativism have formed the subject matter of several recent publications. The most original and stimulating is Charles S. Maier's *Recasting Bourgeois Europe: Stabilization in France, Ger-*

many, and Italy in the Decade after World War I (Princeton, 1975), wherein is delineated a supranational pattern of change away from government by traditional parliamentary means and toward "corporatist" representation and control by economic interest groups. On the unmistakable left-wing origins of Fascist Italian corporativism, Jack J. Roth, *The Cult of Violence: Sorel and the Sorelians* (Berkeley, 1980), considers the influence of the founder of syndicalist socialism to whom Mussolini acknowledged a sizeable debt. *The Syndicalist Tradition and Italian Fascism* (Chapel Hill, 1979) by David D. Roberts is an excellent study of those Italian petty bourgeois intellectuals who moved from belief in a Marxist proletarian uprising, through syndicalism, to endorsement of Fascism's corporative revolution from above. A. J. Gregor, however, in *Young Mussolini and the Intellectual Origins of Fascism* (Berkeley, 1979) strains credulity by insisting that the Duce, almost throughout his public career, was a consistent syndicalist and corporativist thinker. The ideological role played by corporativism is highlighted by Edward R. Tannenbaum, "The Goals of Italian Fascism," *American Historical Review*, LXXIV (1969), 1183–1204; Roland Sarti, "Fascist Modernization in Italy," *ibid.*, LXXV (1970), 1029–45, intimates how corporativism responded to the "productivist" dream of bringing Italy into the twentieth century. Sarti has also written an incisive account of the abiding power of the *Confindustria* under Mussolini:—*Fascism and the Industrial Leadership in Italy* (Berkeley, 1971). On agriculture in Fascist Italy, the standard critique is Carl T. Schmidt, *The Plough and the Sword* (New York, 1938), which may be supplemented by Paul Corner, "Fascist Agrarian Policy and the Italian Economy in the Interwar Years," in *Gramsci and Italy's Passive Revolution*, edited by John A. Davies (London, 1979), pp. 239–74.

Since the close of the Second World War, scholars have intermittently addressed themselves to the large question of the totalitarian character of Italian Fascism. Dante L. Germino in his study of the P.N.F., *The Italian Fascist Party in Power* (Minneapolis, 1959), accepts Mussolini's totalitarian boast at face value. But the skepticism of most social scientists is epitomized in Hannah Arendt's *Origins of Totalitarianism*, 2d ed. (New York, 1958). The most authoritative refutation of Fascist totalitarianism, however, is provided by Alberto Aquarone, *L'organizzazione dello Stato totalitario* (Turin, 1965), who stresses the regime's incontrovertible failure to supplant Italy's traditional power structure. For illustration of this from opposite ends of the social scale, consult Robert Katz on the Italian monarchy, *The Fall of the House of Savoy* (New York, 1971), and Jack E. Reece, "Fascism, the Mafia, and the Emergence of Sicilian separatism, 1919–1943," *Journal of Modern History*, XLV (1973), 261–76.

Of all institutions which preserved a degree of autonomy under Fascism, the Catholic church has attracted most attention. A very judicious and detailed study is by Daniel A. Binchy, *Church and State in Fascist Italy* (New York, 1941). Binchy is not uncritical of the papacy, but a sharper attack on the Vatican for compromising with Fascism in the Lateran Accords is delivered by Carlo Arturo Jemolo in his more general work, *Church and State in Italy, 1850–1950* (Oxford, 1960). The main theme of Richard A. Webster's *The Cross and the Fasces* (Stanford, 1960) is the preservation of the Christian Democratic movement under Fascism. The foundation of a Catholic political party and the uphill struggle of its first leader, Don Luigi Sturzo, against early Fascism are the concern of John N. Molony, *The Emergence of Political Catholicism in Italy: Partito Popolare, 1919–1926* (London, 1977). Elisa A. Carillo, *Alcide De Gasperi: The Long Apprenticeship* (Notre Dame, 1965), deals with the next Christian Democratic leader's clandestine role in the later Fascist era.

The primacy of propaganda in Mussolini's eyes makes Philip V. Cannistraro's study of the Ministry of Popular Culture, *La fabbrica del consenso: Fascismo e mass media* (Bari, 1975), an important as well as a solid monograph. Victoria De Grazia, *The Culture of Consent: Mass Organization of Leisure in Fascist Italy* (Cambridge, 1981), uses the *Dopolavoro* as a window on Fascism's "low" politics and manipulation of mass opinion. The situation of middle-class feminism in Mussolini's Italy is summarized by Alexander De

Grand, "Women under Italian Fascism," *Historical Journal*, XIV (1976), 947–68. A synopsis of the position of Italy's established intellectual community is Emiliana P. Noether's "Italian Intellectuals under Fascism," *Journal of Modern History*, XLIII (1971), 630–48, while the ambivalent attitude of the younger intelligentsia is also briefly but usefully treated by Michael A. Ledeen, "Italian Fascism and Youth," *Journal of Contemporary History*," IV (July 1969), 137–54. The growing disenchantment with Fascism in the 1930s of the student "generation of the Littoriali" is charted by Ruggero Zangrandi, *Il lungo viaggio attraverso il fascismo* (Milan, 1962), a minor classic based on personal experience. The same theme reappears in an interesting work of documentary fiction by Luigi Preti, *Through the Fascist Fire* (London, 1968).

This last reference may serve as a reminder that historical insights are to be gleaned from a nation's literature. Fortunately, a number of Italian literary works born of the Fascist experience are available in English translation, perhaps the most widely read being Carlo Levi's *Christ Stopped at Eboli* (New York, 1947). This memoir is a brilliant evocation of the torment of a Fascist prisoner sentenced to rural exile and of the condition of the *Mezzogiorno* under Fascism. Among Italian novelists, the most openly political was Ignazio Silone, who spent most of the Fascist years in exile. His most celebrated anti-Fascist books, *Fontamara* (New York, 1934) and *Bread and Wine* (New York, 1937), depict the Italian people bearing the Fascist yoke with stoic resignation. Silone is most knowledgeable about villages, Vasco Pratolini about towns. The latter's *A Tale of Poor Lovers* (New York, 1949) is set in Florence where Fascism compels even the most apolitical workers to take sides. Alberto Moravia's first novel, *The Time of Indifference* (New York, 1953), conveys the ennui of the Roman upper middle class in the 1920s; some interpret the title as symbolic of the majority of Italians' refusal to give full emotional commitment to Fascism. A more recent novel well worth commendation is Giorgio Bassani, *The Garden of the Finzi-Continis* (New York, 1965), a sensitively told tale of a cultured Italian Jewish family trapped by the official anti-Semitism of latter-day Fascism.

The place of united Italy in international affairs is satisfactorily surveyed by Cedric J. Lowe and Frank Marzari, *Italian Foreign Policy, 1870–1940* (London, 1975), although the book has some rough edges because of the untimely death of both authors before publication. Overviews of Mussolinian diplomacy begin with Gaetano Salvemini, *Prelude to World War II* (New York, 1954), a revised English edition of *Mussolini diplomatico, 1922–1932* (Paris, 1932). Salvemini dismisses Fascist foreign policy as totally incoherent, as does Denis Mack Smith in his anecdotal but more up-to-date *Mussolini's Roman Empire* (London, 1976). An apologia for Mussolini's actions abroad is Luigi Villari, *Italian Foreign Policy under Mussolini* (New York, 1956). Relations between Italy's Foreign Ministry and Fascism form the subject of two essays in *The Diplomats, 1919–1939*, edited by Gordon A. Craig and Felix Gilbert (Princeton, 1953). H. Stuart Hughes, "The Early Diplomacy of Italian Fascism," pp. 210–33, somewhat exaggerates the restraining influence of the Italian career diplomats in the twenties; Felix Gilbert, "Ciano and his Ambassadors," pp. 512–36, gives a good appraisal of the *fascistizzazione* of the foreign service after 1936.

A fair body of specialist writing on aspects and episodes of Fascist Italy's foreign policy by now exists. The rise and fall of Fascism itself was mirrored in the story of Italy's northeastern provinces acquired at the end of World War I; the confrontation with Germans and Slavs is set out in orderly fashion by Dennison I. Rusinow, *Italy's Austrian Heritage, 1919–1946* (New York, 1969). Alan Cassels, *Mussolini's Early Diplomacy* (Princeton, 1970), denies that the 1920s were a "decade of good behavior" by Fascist Italy in world affairs. *The Pope and the Duce* (London, 1981) by Peter C. Kent discusses the limited impact of the Lateran Accords on Italian foreign policy. Konrad H. Jarausch, *The Four Power Pact, 1933* (Madison, 1965), is a systematic account of Mussolini's abortive effort to bring Hitler's Germany within a new concert of Europe. The European balance which provided opportunity for Fascism's attack on Ethiopia is the core of Esmonde M. Robertson's *Mussolini as Empire-Builder: Europe and Africa, 1932–1936* (London, 1977).

The most comprehensive treatment of this turning point in Fascist diplomacy is found in George Baer's two titles, *The Coming of the Italian-Ethiopian War* (New York, 1966) and *Test Case: Italy, Ethiopia, and the League of Nations* (Stanford, 1976). Baer ascribes Mussolini's Ethiopian venture mainly to domestic factors, although without offering much firm evidence; on Italy and the League of Nations, however, he is authoritative. Frank M. Hardie, *The Abyssinian Crisis* (London, 1974), is a straightforward overall account, and A. J. Barker, *The Civilizing Mission* (London, 1968), concentrates on the military side of the Italo-Ethiopian war. Another Italian interest in Africa is well covered by Claudio G. Segrè, *Fourth Shore: The Italian Colonization of Libya* (Chicago, 1965). Fascist Italy's costly entanglement in Spain is detailed in John F. Coverdale's *Italian Intervention in the Spanish Civil War* (Princeton, 1975), which is stronger on events in Spain than on policy-making in Italy. Opinion outside Italy was, until 1936, often well disposed to Italian Fascism. Alastair Hamilton, *The Appeal of Fascism* (London, 1971), deals with intellectual and artistic sympathizers, while John P. Diggins, *Mussolini and Fascism: The View from America* (Princeton, 1972), embraces a broad social spectrum in the United States.

Every one of the numerous works on the Rome-Berlin Axis relies to a greater or lesser extent on Ciano's celebrated diary, published in English in two volumes: *The Ciano Diaries, 1939–1943* (New York, 1946) and *Ciano's Hidden Diaries, 1937–1938* (London, 1952). Ciano's frankness in print stands in sharp contrast to the circumspection of most diplomatic memoirs. On Ciano himself there is no English-language biography; the most recent from Italy is by Giordano B. Guerri, *Galeazzo Ciano, una vita 1903–1944* (Milan, 1979). A pioneering monograph on the Axis is Elizabeth Wiskemann's *Rome-Berlin Axis*, rev. ed. (London, 1969), heavily factual and now dated. The transformation of Axis into alliance is related by Mario Toscano, *The Origins of the Pact of Steel* (Baltimore, 1967), a definitive account in terms of old-fashioned diplomatic history. In reality, of course, the Axis and the Pact of Steel were anything but examples of conventional "cabinet politics"; on the contrary, they operated on various levels of understanding, which is the point of D. C. Watt's article, "The Rome-Berlin Axis, 1936–1940: Myth and Reality," *Review of Politics*, XXII (1960), 519–43. The Axis had social consequences, too, notably the introduction of anti-Semitism into Fascist Italy. Meir Michaelis, *Mussolini and the Jews* (Oxford, 1978), is a work of vast scholarship. While admitting the potent influence of the Axis in this question, Michaelis proves that Hitler did not force anti-Semitism on Mussoini; moreover, his researches have uncovered a lot of latent anti-Semitism in early Fascism. Gene Bernardini, "Origins and Development of Racial Anti-Semitism in Fascist Italy," *Journal of Modern History*, XLIX (1977), 431–53, discusses Mussolini's claim to have invented a uniquely Italian Fascist form of racism.

Mussolini's lurch into the Second World War concludes Rosaria Quartararo's important and detailed *Roma tra Londra e Berlino: Politica estera fascista dal 1930 al 1940* (Rome, 1980). This is an exposition of the view that Mussolini was trying to steer an equidistant course between the power blocs as late as the spring of 1940. On the other hand, the Duce of MacGregor Knox's *Mussolini Unleashed, 1939–1941* (New York, 1980) is less statesmanlike; rather, he was brutally set on war as a means of drastically altering Italian national character and society. The unpopularity of the Second World War among Italians at large is concisely stated by Alberto Aquarone, "Lo spirito pubblico in Italia alla vigilia della seconda guerra mondiale," *Nord e Sud*, XI (Jan. 1964), 117–25.

The dismal performance of Italian Fascism on the battlefield is exemplified in Mario Cervi, *The Hollow Legions: Mussolini's Blunders in Greece, 1940–1941* (London, 1972). This record, in turn, brought on the vote of no confidence in Mussolini's leadership in the Fascist Grand Council session of July 24 and 25, 1943. The Duce's own account of these events, *The Fall of Mussolini* (New York, 1948), may be set against Grandi's version, *Dino Grandi racconta* (Venice, 1945), excerpts from which appeared in English in the American magazine, *Life*, on February 26, 1945. The authoritative story of Mussolini's fall and subsequent resurrection as head of the Salò Republic is contained in Sir F. William Deakin, *The Brutal Friendship* (London, 1962), an apt title to describe Mussolini's subservience to Hitler from 1942 to 1945. Deakin's is a magisterial work based on Mussolini's private papers. It does not relate the details of the Duce's flight and death in 1945, but these can be ascertained in Roman Dombrowski, *Mussolini—Twilight and Fall* (New York, 1956). The travail of Italians living in the Salò Republic and subject to Nazi brutality is illustrated by Robert Katz, *Death in Rome* (New York, 1967). This is a record of the notorious execution in the Ardeatine Caves of 335 Italian hostages in reprisal for partisan activity. The anti-Fascist resistance came into its own, of course, between 1943 and 1945. The standard work on the development of resistance to Fascism over twenty years as well as the partisans' role against Salò is Charles F. Delzell, *Mussolini's Enemies* (Princeton, 1961). This may be supplemented by Frank Rosengarten, *The Italian Anti-Fascist Press, 1919–1945* (Cleveland, 1968).

It remains to mention a few of the many works which have attempted the vexed task of relating Mussolini's movement to *universalfascismo* or fascism at large. The Marxian school of thought has never been at a loss for a typology of fascism; everything is explicable within the contours of capitalism and class. Nevertheless, such a frame of reference does not preclude subtlety and acute observation—witness *Lectures on Fascism* (New York, 1976) by Palmiro Togliatti, the Italian Communist leader during the Fascist era. For a specimen of updated and sophisticated Marxist scholarship, see Nicos Poulantzas, *Fascism and Dictatorship* (London, 1974). An enduring theory of the middle-class basis of fascism is found in Seymour Lipset's *Political Man*, rev. ed. (New York, 1981), where the author defines his term "extremism of the center." The seminal work in the ongoing debate over *universalfascismo*, however, is Ernst Nolte, *Three Faces of Fascism: Action Française, Italian Fascism, National Socialism* (New York, 1966). In this very ambitious and abstruse book Nolte finds a common denominator in the "anti-transcendental" nature of his three fascist case studies. But the model seems tailored to fit the peculiar characteristics of Nazism, and the explanation of Italian Fascism as a return to elemental primitivism does not carry conviction. In reply to Nolte, Renzo De Felice's *Interpretations of Fascism* (Cambridge, Mass., 1977) emphasizes the intrinsic differences between the Mussolinian and Hitlerian world views. A long and interpretative article by MacGregor Knox, "Conquest, Foreign and Domestic, in Fascist Italy and Nazi Germany," *Journal of Modern History*, LVI (1984), 1–57, assays a balance. While recognizing distinctions between the objective situations within which Italian Fascism and German Nazism developed, it finds common ground in the indissoluble linking of revolution at home and expansion abroad in both Mussolini's and Hitler's thought. Another effort to schematize parallels and dissimilarities in the Italian and German experiences, along with other Fascist episodes, is Alan Cassels, *Fascism* (Arlington Heights, Ill., 1975); modesty forbids any word on the book's viability. This author perceives two fascist prototypes emerging out of a common revolt against the nineteenth-century order, but once in power pursuing separate aims—rational corporativism and primordial racism, respectively—according to the different degree of modernization achieved in each nation. Such dichotomy between two species of fascism was brought into the open by the abortive experiment of a fascist international, described by Michael A. Ledeen in his *Universal Fascism: The Theory and Practice of the Fascist International, 1928–1936* (New York, 1972). The appeal of Mussolini's prototypical fascism to backward, rather than modern, communities is illustrated further by Charles F. Delzell's documentary publication, *Mediterranean Fascism* (New York, 1971). The equation of generic fascism with a series of developmental dictatorships, including Bolshevik Russia and Castro's Cuba, is an *idée fixe* of all A. J. Gregor's books; it may be sampled in his *Italian Fascism and Developmental Dictatorship* (Princeton, 1979). This and other outlandish variations on the fascist theme are pilloried by Gilbert Allardyce, "What Fascism

Is Not; Thoughts on the Deflation of a Concept," *American Historical Review*, LXXXIV (1979), 367–98.

The foregoing constitutes no more than a selective bibliography. For further reference, Charles F. Delzell, *Italy in the Twentieth Century*, American Historical Association Pamphlet 428 (Washington, 1980), is strongly recommended. Also in the bibliographical realm, Howard M. Smyth's *Secrets of the Fascist Era* (Carbondale, 1975) is a lively account of the recovery of much of the primary source material of Mussolini's Italy.

Index